Camping Illinois

A Comprehensive Guide to the State's Best Campgrounds

Ted Villaire

FALCONGUIDES

GUILFORD, CONNECTICUT
HELENA, MONTANA

AN IMPRINT OF GLOBE PEQUOT PRESS

FALCONGUIDES®

Copyright © 2010 by Morris Book Publishing, LLC

FalconGuides is an imprint of Globe Pequot Press.

Falcon, FalconGuides, and Outfit Your Mind are registered trademarks of Morris Book Publishing, LLC.

Project editor: David Legere
Layout artist: Sue Murray
Maps by Trailhead Graphics © Morris Book Publishing LLC.

Interior photos by Ted Villaire unless otherwise noted.

Library of Congress Cataloging-in-Publication Data is available on file.

ISBN 978-0-7627-4690-3

Printed in the United States of America

10 9 8 7 6 5 4 3 2 1

Contents

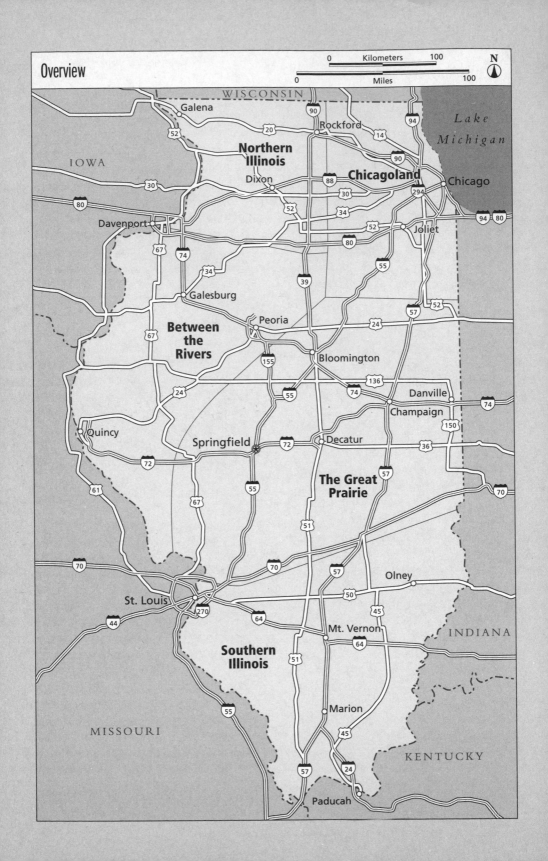

Acknowledgments

I have a mountain of gratitude directed toward the staff of the many public campgrounds in Illinois. Despite repeated belt-tightening measures, they still find time to enthusiastically promote their parks and share their deep well of knowledge with visitors. In particular, I want to thank the rangers and volunteer campground hosts serving Illinois state parks. These people fulfill the important need of maintaining the natural treasures of Illinois and ensuring that visitors have an enjoyable visit. Researching this book and traveling solo around Illinois for weeks at a time made me starved for human contact. As a result, I was the mildly annoying guy asking a million questions while the park ranger or host patiently recited his or her answers and indulged me in a bit of chitchat. I would like to thank Mike Williams, a site technician at Moraine View State Park, who brought skill, patience, and a jolly demeanor to the task of retrieving my keys after I brilliantly locked them in my rental car. A special thanks to Johnny Molloy, a terrific guidebook writer who got me started in writing outdoor recreation guidebooks by offering encouragement and connecting me with book editors. Finally, I would like to express thanks to my friends and family members who offered support while I researched and wrote the book.

Introduction

People unfamiliar with Illinois may think that the state offers little to see outside of the urban areas. They may think it's all flat cropland, and they may assume the parks and natural areas are unimpressive. These misconceptions are immediately laid to rest once they start to explore the state. While it's true that glaciers steamrolled much of the land, exceptions to the flat landscape are everywhere. These include the hills in northwest Illinois and the entire south tip of the state. Don't forget the hills in northern Chicagoland or the wooded bluffs that run for miles along the Mississippi River. Or the sandstone canyons along the Illinois and Big Muddy Rivers. Or the dozens of pockets of rugged woodland peppered throughout the state, often where parks have been established. The list could continue.

Along with the glaciers, the rivers are the other major force that shaped the landscape in Illinois. Indeed, Illinois is fortunate to have several major rivers, including the Mississippi, the Illinois, and the Ohio. These major waterways, which may swell to 2 to 3 miles wide in places, contain locks, dams, and barge traffic. Outside their banks, particularly along the Illinois and Mississippi Rivers, wooded bluffs and vast swaths of bottomland and wetland offer many thousands of acres of recreational opportunities.

Hundreds of tiny to enormous lakes also model the Illinois landscape. Even though nearly all the state's lakes south of Chicago are human-made artifacts, visitors will be surprised by the scenic and peaceful atmosphere at these places. Wooded shores, hidden inlets, plenty of birdlife, and a typically remote atmosphere offer great opportunities for escape. People come to these lakes in search of game fish such as bass, crappie, catfish, walleye, and trout. They also come to camp. They come to launch their boats, they come for shoreside lounging, and they come for hiking.

Along with boating, fishing, and hiking, one of the most popular outdoor activities is watching wildlife. Deer, raccoons, woodchucks, turkeys, and foxes are common sights in Illinois. Less frequently you may encounter bobcats, coyotes, and beavers. Bird-watchers will delight in the number of hawks, woodpeckers, and songbirds. Sandhill cranes show up occasionally, and great blue herons are everywhere. In the winter, bald eagles descend on the major rivers looking for open water. Illinois is fortunate to be in a central position on the migration route for millions of birds every spring and fall. About 250 bird species use the Mississippi Flyway, as it's called, in the spring from mid-March to early June, and in autumn from late August to late October. During these seasons, migratory birds show up at the scores of lakes and wetlands around the state and along the shores of the rivers.

Many people find camping in spring and fall appealing because this is when campgrounds are quieter, the bugs are dormant, and there's no chance of encountering extreme heat. Some people time their camping trip to coincide with the vibrant colors of fall or with festivals that focus on local food and crafts. The Illinois State Fair in late August has a reputation as one of the best state fairs in the Midwest. There's live entertainment, miles of food booths and livestock displays, and races to watch from the grandstand.

In addition to outdoor recreation and seasonal events, Illinois possesses a variety of cultural offerings. Numerous museums and historical sites honor Illinois' most famous son, Abraham Lincoln. Chicago, of course, claims some of the best museums in the world, and nearly every county in the state has a small museum or historical society that will give you a taste of life in the state's early days. Small historic river towns such as Nauvoo, Galena, and Alton offer a glimpse of life when big rivers served as the nation's superhighways.

Overall, there's no shortage of reasons to explore Illinois. Even when you get beyond a mere introduction and become well acquainted with the state, it'll continue to charm you with its rich history, scenic landscapes, and easy conversations with its friendly and gracious residents.

Great efforts were undertaken to ensure the accuracy and usefulness of the information in this book. With a handful of exceptions, I visited each campground listed. The visits usually included a survey of the park's offerings beyond the campground. I inspected the showers and restrooms, visited the picnic areas, and dropped in at visitor centers. In a number of cases, I hiked the trails offered near the campground and investigated nearby towns and attractions. Despite thousands of miles of travel and many weeks of legwork, a perfectly accurate guidebook remains elusive. Inevitably, campgrounds become run-down, they close, they are renovated, new ones open, and services and policies change. If you find any inaccuracies in the book, please let me know so that future editions can be improved. Send corrections to editorial@ GlobePequot.com or to Ted Villaire c/o Globe Pequot Press, P.O. Box 480, Guilford, CT, 06437.

How to Use This Guide

The focus of this book is on public campgrounds. For people interested in exploring scenic landscapes and enjoying the full spectrum of outdoor recreation opportunities, public campgrounds have the most to offer in Illinois. While there's nothing wrong with the resortlike atmosphere common in private campgrounds, that is the subject of a different book.

Types of Campgrounds

The easiest way to categorize campgrounds is by management agency. Nearly all the campgrounds in the state can fit into the following categories.

Federal: All Illinois campgrounds operated by the National Forest Service are located within the sprawling Shawnee National Forest. Most of these campgrounds are basic, and some are operated by concessionaires. (In addition to formal campsites, this federal site also offers primitive camping throughout the forest at least a quarter mile from campgrounds and picnic areas, and at least 150 feet from trails.) The Illinois campgrounds operated by the U.S. Army Corps of Engineers are always located along lakes and waterways where the Corps owns land.

State: The State of Illinois operates the most public campgrounds in the state—about eighty. Its state parks, recreation areas, and historic sites are generally more developed than the campsites in fish and wildlife and conservation areas.

County: Some readers may be unaware of the great variety of county-operated campgrounds throughout the state. Many of these campgrounds occupy scenic spots near lakes, rivers, and woodland. In many cases, these campgrounds are little known outside their immediate areas.

Local: Illinois contains a large collection of campgrounds owned by local municipalities. These campgrounds, often located in town parks, tend to be small, have limited facilities, and attract mostly local campers. Since many of them are located close to a town, they are particularly handy for visitors who want a convenient location from which to explore nearby attractions.

Locating a Campground

To help you choose a campground, the book is organized roughly according to the state regions determined by the Illinois Bureau of Tourism. Maps within the book show the location of each campground within these regions. Each region is broken into areas. In each area, the campgrounds are listed alphabetically. By consulting the regional maps and scanning the campground descriptions, you can select a campground that appeals to your interests and fits best with your travel plans.

About the Campground Entries

Each campground description covers the following information.

Location: Here we help you get your general bearings with distance and direction from a town nearby.

Season: While the typical operating season for each campground is listed, it's never a bad idea to call first to make sure a campground is open when you plan to arrive. Campgrounds can close unexpectedly for maintenance, modifications, and soggy ground. Illinois contains many riverside campgrounds that may close because of flooding in spring, or even in summer. And once floodwaters recede, a great deal of cleanup must occur. Strained park budgets and limited staff can prolong the cleanup process, sometimes for the entire season. Another reason to call the campground before arriving is to find out if hunters will be present. Many state parks allow hunting in fall and winter.

Among the many of the campgrounds that stay open year-round, you should assume that water, showers, and flush toilets will not be available for campers during the winter. While exceptions to this rule exist, it's better to be prepared by bringing your own water.

Sites: Each campground description gives the number of sites for RVs (with and without hookups), the number of sites available for tenting, and the number of walk-in sites (also for tenting). Sites without hookups are basic sites that will accommodate either an RV or a tent. RV refers to the many types of recreational vehicles on the road: trailers, campers, motor homes, tent trailers, and vans. Under this heading, there will also be a listing of cabins to rent, as well as an indication of wheelchair-accessible sites available. Walk-in sites require a short walk—usually no more then 50 yards—from the parking area. A few of the camping areas require a longer trek; in these cases, the general distance is given. Backpacking sites require a long hike.

Maximum length: Each campground entry gives the maximum length for RVs so you can be sure your rig will fit. Most campgrounds in Illinois can accommodate 40-foot RVs. Some of the smaller campgrounds or campgrounds with tight, winding roads will place greater restrictions on RV length. Generally, the larger the campground, the more likely it will accommodate a larger RV.

Facilities: This is the place to find out if a park contains showers, a boat launch, a playground, hiking trails, or any number of other offerings. With just a few exceptions, all the campgrounds listed in this book provide drinking water. This section will alert you if a campground does not offer drinking water.

Fee per night: The price codes used throughout the book are from fall 2009. A range is used because prices fluctuate from year to year.

$ = Less than $10

$$ = $10 to $19

$$$ = $20 or more

When the price indicates a wide range ($–$$$), expect the tenting and basic sites to cost less and hookup sites to cost more. The prices listed don't reflect the cost of cabins or the rental tents that are offered at a dozen or so state parks. Nor do they reflect fee increases that occur at some campgrounds on holiday weekends, such as Memorial Day, Fourth of July, and Labor Day. (The State of Illinois recently increased the cost for camping on holiday weekends; check out the fee structure at http://dnr.state.il.us and click on camping.)

Management: This section lists the federal, state, or local agency that maintains and collects fees for the campground.

Contact: This is where contact information for the management agency is provided. If reservations are accepted for a campground, this section will provide that information. Reservations are a good idea if you're going to be camping over a holiday weekend, or if you are visiting a park with a reputation for being fairly busy (Large state parks in the Chicago area all tend to be busy on summer weekends). You also may want to make reservations if there is an event in the area, or if there are no alternative campgrounds in the immediate area and your travel plans hinge on local camping. If in doubt whether to reserve or not, call the park and talk to a park ranger. He or she will offer sound advice on the necessity of reservations for a particular date.

In the state park system, reservations are made through the individual park and must be mailed or dropped off in person (no e-mail reservations accepted). Reservations require the first night's camping fee as well as a nonrefundable $5 reservation fee. Some parks have their own reservation form and others use a generic form (visit http://dnr.state.il.us and click on camping to find the downloadable forms). If reservations are accepted at campgrounds operated by the U.S. Army Corps of Engineers, make the reservations by visiting www.recreation.gov (click reservation policies at the bottom of the screen) or by calling (877) 444-6777. For the county and local campgrounds that accept reservations, contact the local management agency.

Finding the campground: Using an atlas or local maps in conjunction with the driving directions provided in this section will help you find your way to the campgrounds listed in this book. Directions guide you from the closest interstate or the closest city or larger town. The *Illinois Atlas & Gazetteer,* published by Delorme, is indispensable in navigating rural back roads of Illinois.

UTM coordinates: Readers who use either a handheld or car-mounted GPS unit can punch in the UTM campground coordinates provided in this section and have the GPS lead the way. The UTM coordinates are to be used with NAD 27 datum (rather than WGS83 or WGS84). Along with the UTM coordinates, the zone is also given. All coordinates were generated using mapping software, rather than taking readings "in the field." In nearly all cases, the UTM coordinates will take you directly to the campground. In a few cases, the coordinates will lead you to the park entrance or the park office.

About the campground: This section describes the physical atmosphere of the campground, including the topography, the amount of greenery and shade, and levels of privacy within the sites. You'll get a quick account of the campground's ambience and its proximity to lakes, rivers, busy roads, and nearby towns. You'll also learn about local offerings, such as hiking trails and areas of historical interest.

Amenities Charts Key:

Hookup Sites
Total Sites

Max RV Length: All RV lengths are in feet.

Hookups:

W	=	Water
E	=	Electricity
S	=	Sewer

Toilets:

F	=	Flush toilets
NF	=	Non-flushing toilets

Showers:

N	=	None
Y	=	Yes

Drinking Water:

N	=	None
Y	=	Yes

Dump Station:

N	=	None
Y	=	Yes

Recreation:

H	=	Hiking
S	=	Swimming
F	=	Fishing
B	=	Boating
L	=	Boat launch
O	=	Off-road driving
R	=	Horseback riding
C	=	Cycling

Fee: $
       $$
       $$$

Reservations:

N	=	None
Y	=	Yes

Conscientious Camping

Careful planning plus appreciation and respect for the natural world are key components of a great outdoor experience. The listings below are offered to guide you toward a fun camping trip that's easy on you, on the environment, and keeps you safe too.

Respecting the Environment

Zero-impact camping should be the goal of everyone. When you leave a campground it should look better than when you arrived.

Campfires: Heed all regulations concerning campfires, smoking, and wood gathering. To prevent the spread of the emerald ash borer insect, you should know the rules restricting the transportation of firewood. If you live in the eighteen-county area of northeastern Illinois or in certain parts of Michigan, Indiana, and Ohio, you may not bring firewood from home. Instead, you must acquire firewood locally. (Most campgrounds offer some nearby options for purchasing firewood). Visit www.emerald ashborer.info to see what parts of the Midwest have firewood quarantines.

Courtesy: Please keep your campground clean and show respect for other campers who want to enjoy a tranquil atmosphere. Keep the sound level low, especially during quiet hours. Generally, people don't camp in order to listen to your recorded music or to listen to your generator at all hours. With cutbacks at many parks, fewer park staff are on hand to patrol the grounds and ask people to turn down the music. As a result, campers must regulate themselves.

Storing food: During times you're away from the site and during the night, store food in your car; otherwise, squirrels, raccoons, and chipmunks will steal your provisions. If you don't have a car at the campsite, bring food inside the tent or hang it from a tree.

Garbage: If no trash containers are provided, pack it out. At night and when you are away from the campsite, stash your trash in your vehicle. Never toss garbage into the vault toilets or leave it behind in the fire pit.

Sanitation: Bathing and dishwashing should be done well away from lakes and streams and away from the campground's water supplies.

Smoking: To prevent fires, use extreme care when smoking. Dispose of butts properly or pack them out.

Pets: Keep your animal at your site, restrained and quiet. On trails, pets must be leashed at all times to protect wildlife and habitat.

Stay limits: Public campgrounds typically have stay limits ranging from a few days to two weeks. Some campgrounds offer longer stays.

Getting Geared Up

Clothing: Since Illinois is nearly 400 miles from head to toe, its climate can vary considerably. As one would suspect, the normal camping season is extended in the south (as are the hot and sticky days of midsummer), and is a bit shorter in the north. While camping during spring and fall, you want to be prepared for a full spectrum of weather conditions.

Wool makes the most versatile clothing and works great for cold, wet, changeable weather. It retains heat even when it's wet and it does not absorb smells as readily as other fabrics. Cotton is the fabric for warm summer days. Shorts are great for warm summer days, too, but you'll likely want a pair of long pants in the evening when the mosquitoes emerge. Always bring along a rain jacket.

Footwear: Sneakers are appropriate for most activities while camping in Illinois. Where there's likely to be mud or more rugged trails—in the Shawnee National Forest, for example—boots are a better option. They provide support and protection from the elements and rocky surface.

Equipment: Your quantity and variety of camping gear will depend on the time of year, your destination, and the level of comfort that you prefer. Along with a tent, sleeping bags, food, and a flashlight, you may want to bring items such as a gas stove, lantern, and large water container. Some campers bring extra items that add to their comfort: a hammock, a small weather radio, and a tarp to hang above the picnic table to block the rain and sun. If you plan to hike, be sure to bring a daypack with padded straps to carry items such as snacks, water, raingear, an extra sweater, keys, money, sunglasses, a camera, and binoculars.

Once you start wading through the options for camping gear, you'll encounter a bewildering number of possibilities. One rule of thumb is to keep the packing list as simple as you can. When it's easy to pack and make your escape, you're likely to do it more often. The key is to bring just enough gear to make your stay safe and comfortable. While that list will be different for everyone, keep in mind that bringing too much stuff tends to complicate the experience and may defeat the purpose of escaping to the woods.

Staying Safe

Many of these campgrounds are in fairly remote areas, sometimes a good distance away from towns, hospitals, and stores. As a result, campers should be prepared for various possibilities with a first-aid kit and a supply of food and water. If you own a cell phone, it's likely that you'll have reception at most Illinois campgrounds. While cell phones are convenient, they are no replacement for being thoroughly prepared.

Water: Avoid drinking from streams in Illinois—even if you use a water purifier. Outside of urban areas, most streams in Illinois contain agricultural run-off, which may contain waste from grazing animals as well as fertilizers and pesticides used in agricultural production.

Hypothermia: Hypothermia occurs when your body temperature drops to a dangerous level. Common causes are exposure to cold, physical exhaustion, and too little food. Contributing factors may include exposure to wind, rain and snow, dehydration, and wearing damp or wet clothes. Falling in cold water on a cool day is one of the fastest ways to make your body temperature plummet.

Poison Ivy: A nasty encounter with poison ivy can put a damper on your outdoor vacation. Poison ivy is a very common plant throughout most of Illinois. It occurs as a vine or groundcover, three leaflets to a leaf, and contains urushiol, an oily and toxic irritant that is responsible for the skin rash. After contact, raised lines or blisters will occur on the skin. Do not scratch it. Wash and dry the surface, then apply calamine lotion to dry it out. If the case is severe, consult a doctor.

Stings and Bites: Most often, mosquitoes and other biting insects are more of a nuisance than a danger. Using insect repellant, wearing pants and long sleeves, and avoiding areas where the insects congregate all are strategies to keep from getting bitten.

If you're spending ample time outdoors, you should know about the diseases spread by some insects. Individuals can become infected by the West Nile virus if bitten by an infected mosquito. Culex mosquitoes, the primary varieties that can transmit West Nile virus to humans, thrive in urban rather than natural areas. Insect repellant and protective clothing are the best preventive measures. Remember to follow instructions on the insect repellant, especially when applying it to children.

Ticks are often found on brush and tall grass waiting to catch a ride on a warm-blooded passerby. While they're most active in early and midsummer, you should keep an eye peeled for them throughout spring, summer, and fall. Deer ticks, the primary carrier of Lyme disease, are very small, sometimes only the size of a poppy seed. For hikers, one of the most common places to find ticks is inside the top edge of your sock (ticks need some type of backstop to start drilling into the skin). Some people wear light clothing so they can spot ticks right away. Insect repellant containing DEET is an effective deterrent. Most importantly, be sure to visually check yourself, especially if you're out on a hike. If it's prime tick season, you'll want to check your exposed skin (particularly your legs, if you're wearing shorts) every hour or so, and then do a more thorough examination back in your tent or in the shower. For ticks that are already embedded, tweezers work best for removal.

Map Legend

Transportation

- Interstate Highway (90)
- U.S. Highway (40)
- State Highway (16)

Symbols

- Campground (30)
- Capital
- City
- State Line (ILLINOIS / MISSOURI)

Hydrology

- Body of Water
- River

Land Use

- National Forest

Scale: 0 Kilometers 20 / 0 Miles 20

True North: N

Northern Illinois

Norr and north central Illinois offer plenty of diversions for travelers and outdoor explorers. For good reason, the town of Galena sits near the top of most local tourism itineraries. This small historic town near the Mississippi River is chock-full of restaurants, shops, and attractive historic architecture. Galena claims a few museums, including one devoted to its most famous resident, Ulysses S. Grant. What the throngs of visitors to Galena often fail to fully experience is the countryside surrounding the town. Hands down, it's the most scenic terrain in northern Illinois. The big hills and valleys, small dairy farms, lush woodland, and streams flowing through small limestone canyons offer a sharp contrast to the Prairie State's nearby fields of corn and soy. The scenic vistas are enhanced by quiet roads that twist and curve like snakes.

Visitors come to explore the charming towns in the area, but they often come for paddling, fishing, and boating opportunities as well. After the Great Lakes, the premier spot for boating and fishing in this part of the Midwest is the Mississippi River. Between Thomson and Savanna, anglers can explore a 3-mile-wide pool of open water fringed by vast wetlands. Throughout this section of the Mississippi River, islands, wetlands, and backwater lakes are commonplace. The best spot to get a sense of the grandeur of the Upper Mississippi River is from the observation platform on the 250-foot-high river bluffs at Mississippi Palisades State Park. This is one of the most striking views in the entire state. From up here, Old Man River looks like an enormous wetland with large stretches of open water. The river is 2 miles across and includes dozens of islands, fingers of land, and grassy backwater wetlands. Anglers and wildlife watchers can hardly find a better destination in the state.

Many people may not know about the great cycling trails in the area. Cyclists will enjoy the paved path called Great River Trail, which runs along the Mississippi River between Savanna and Fulton and between Albany and the Quad Cities (the Quad Cities include Moline and Rock Island in Illinois and Bettendorf and Davenport in Iowa). Cyclists will also find many miles of peaceful trail riding along the Hennepin Canal Trail, which runs east-west between the Illinois River and the Rock River and north-south between Rock Falls and Mineral.

Another river that runs through this part of the state often fails to get proper acclaim. As the Rock River cuts a path southwest from Rockford toward the Mississippi River, it passes a number of scenic parks and interesting attractions. Winnebago County Forest Preserve District offers a handful of attractive camping options in the vicinity of Rockford. Some of the most interesting places along the Rock River are near the town of Oregon. This is the location of Lowden State Park, which contains a 50-foot concrete sculpture of a Native American perched on a dramatic overlook of the Rock River. Not far away, you'll find a limestone canyon at White Pines State Park and the largest prairie in the state at the Nachusa Grasslands. You can climb high rocky bluffs at Castle Rock State Park and learn about an important chapter in mid-western history at the John Deere Historic Site.

A taste of northern Illinois outdoors would not be complete without a trip to Starved Rock State Park. While Starved Rock is the busiest park in the state, it's also one of the most beguiling. Spend a day exploring the many sandstone canyons that contain streams and waterfalls. From high up on the river bluffs and rocky overlooks, you can see the Illinois River for miles.

The Rockford Area

		Hookup Sites	Total Sites	Max RV Length	Hookups	Toilets	Showers	Drinking Water	Dump Station	Recreation	Fee	Reservations
1	Rock Cut State Park	208	268	45	E	F	Y	Y	Y	H, F, L, C, R, S	$$-$$$	Y
2	Hononegah Forest Preserve	47	60	40	E	F	N	Y	Y	H, F, L	$$	N
3	Sugar River Forest Preserve	63	80	40	E	F	Y	Y	Y	H, F	$$	N
4	Pecatonica River Forest Preserve	49	49	40	E	F	N	Y	Y	H, F, L	$$	N
5	Sumner Park	0	40	35	N/A	F	N	Y	Y	F	$$	N
6	Seward Bluffs Forest Preserve	59	59	40	E	F	Y	Y	Y	H	$$	N

1 Rock Cut State Park

Location: The northeast edge of Rockford
Season: Year-round
Sites: 208 sites with electrical hookups, 60 sites with no hookups
Maximum length: 45 feet
Facilities: Flush toilets, water, showers, tables, grills, dump station, picnic shelters, biking and hiking trails, lakes, boat launch, fishing docks
Fee per night: $$-$$$
Management: Illinois Department of Natural Resources
Contact: (815) 885-3311; http://dnr.state.il.us/lands/landmgt/parks/r1/rockcut.htm; reservations accepted
Finding the campground: On I-39/90 northeast of Rockford, exit west on East Riverside Boulevard. Turn right on North Perryville Road. Several miles ahead, turn right on West Lane Road (IL 173). Enter the park on the right and follow signs to the camping area.
UTM coordinates: 16T, 336672 N, 4690891 E
About the campground: Rock Cut State Park is a large park packed with trails, fishing spots, and picnic areas. In addition to hills, creeks, and a couple of lakes, the park contains large swaths of rehabilitated prairie, where you'll find wildflowers such as compass plants, black-eyed Susans, and goldenrod. The large, well-shaded campground offers some privacy thanks to the shrubs and trees growing between many of the sites. While the park's close proximity to Rockford's suburbs and I-39/90 allows for many local shopping and eating options, it also makes for a somewhat bustling atmosphere.

Northern Illinois

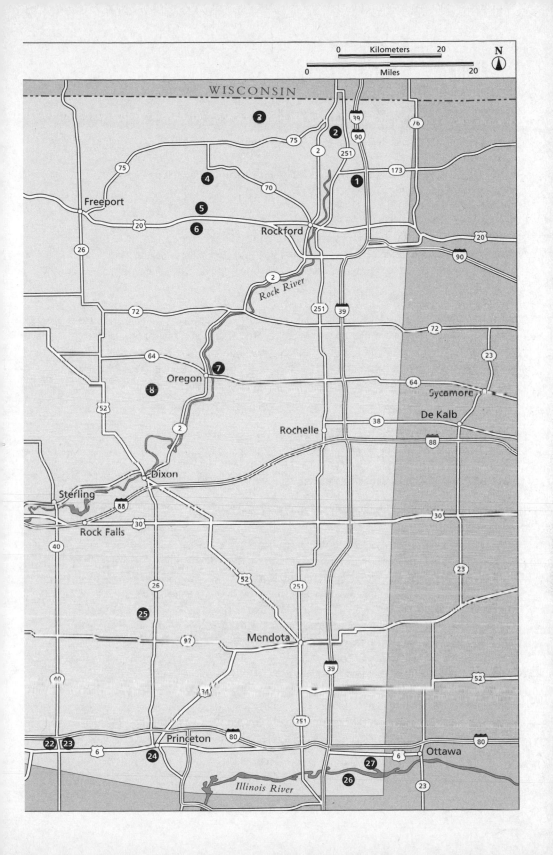

2 Hononegah Forest Preserve

Location: 8 miles north of Rockford
Season: End of Mar to mid-Nov
Sites: 47 sites with electrical hookups, 13 sites with no hookups
Maximum length: 40 feet
Facilities: Flush toilets, grills, water, tables, dump station, picnic shelters, hiking trails, boat launch, pay phone
Fee per night: $$
Management: Winnebago County Forest Preserve District
Contact: (815) 877-6100; http://www.wcfpd.org/preserves/hononegah/
Finding the campground: On I-39/90 northwest of Rockford, exit on East Rockton Road heading west. Turn left on IL 2, and quickly turn left again on Hononegah Road. The entrance to the park is on the right.
UTM coordinates: 16T, 331581 E, 4699989 N
About the campground: The thick stands of oaks create a measure of privacy for the well-spaced sites within this campground. Some of the sites are perched at the top of a small wooded bluff above the meanders of Dry Run Creek. The Rock River is a short walk from the campground. Suburban residential areas border the park, and roads with steady traffic are in the vicinity. Hiking trails run through woodland and alongside the Rock River at this 228-acre park.

3 Sugar River Forest Preserve

Location: About 15 miles northwest of Rockford
Season: End of Mar to mid-Nov
Sites: 63 sites with electrical hookups, 17 sites with no hookups
Maximum length: 40 feet
Facilities: Flush toilets, showers, water, grills, tables, dump station, picnic shelter
Fee per night: $$
Management: Winnebago County Forest Preserve District
Contact: (815) 877-6100; http://www.wcfpd.org/preserves/sugar-river-alder/
Finding the campground: From I-39/90 north of Rockford, exit west on Rockton Road. After passing through Rockton, turn right on Forest Preserve Road. Forest Preserve Road leads directly into the park.
UTM coordinates: 16T, 316024 E, 4704134 N
About the campground: Winnebago County claims an impressive collection of scenic, well-maintained forest preserves. This is one of the best: It contains an attractive campground set within a dense grove of pine trees situated near the Sugar River. The surrounding terrain features prairie, wooded bluffs, and a perfect grassy picnic area beside the winding river. This forest preserve also offers 5.5 miles of hiking trails, as well as a collection of walk-in campsites alongside the river.

A grassy picnicking spot along the Sugar River.

4 Pecatonica River Forest Preserve

Location: About 10 miles west of Rockford
Season: End of Mar to mid-Nov
Sites: 49 sites with electrical hookups
Maximum length: 40 feet
Facilities: Flush toilets, water, grills, tables, dump station, picnic shelter, boat launch, playground
Fee per night: $$
Management: Winnebago County Forest Preserve District
Contact: (815) 877-6100; http://www.wcfpd.org/preserves/pecatonica-river/
Finding the campground: Head northwest of Rockford on IL 70. About 15 miles outside of Rockford, turn left onto Brick School Road. Enter the campground by taking the first park road on the right before Brick School Road curves to the right.
UTM coordinates: 16T 308657E, 4692166 N
About the campground: This forest preserve, which contains an Illinois Nature Preserve, is notable for its wetlands, prairie, and top-notch riverside picnicking grounds. The well-shaded campground is open and compact. Given its out-of-the-way location, it stays quiet most of the season. Nearly 10 miles of hiking trails wind through restored prairie and woodland, next to an oxbow pond and a stone quarry, and alongside the Pecatonica River.

5 Sumner Park

Location: In Pecatonica, 10 miles west of Rockford
Season: Year-round
Sites: 40 sites with no hookups (hookup sites are available at the adjoining Winnebago County Fairgrounds)
Maximum length: 35 feet
Facilities: Flush toilets, water, picnic shelter, sports fields, fairgrounds
Fee per night: $$
Management: Village of Pecatonica
Contact: (815) 239-1555 or (815) 239-2310
Finding the campground: Head west on US 20 from Rockford. Turn right on Jackson Road toward Pecatonica. Turn left into the park just before crossing the Pecatonica River. Camping is available on the riverbank to the right.
UTM coordinates: 16T, 305371 E, 4687515 N
About the campground: This municipal park, steps from downtown Pecatonica, sits alongside the Pecatonica River and the Winnebago County Fairgrounds. The camping area is open, grassy, and minimally shaded. Campers sometimes pitch a tent here while paddling this stretch of the Pecatonica River. Across the river is the 1,000-acre Pecatonica Wetlands Forest Preserve containing bottomland forest and oxbow pond marshes. In Pecatonica, you can also explore the Pecatonica Prairie Path, a rough-surfaced rail-trail.

6 Seward Bluffs Forest Preserve

Location: About 15 miles west of Rockford
Season: End of Mar to mid-Nov
Sites: 59 sites with electrical hookups
Maximum length: 40 feet
Facilities: Flush toilets, showers, grills, water, tables, dump station, picnic shelter
Fee per night: $$
Management: Winnebago County Forest Preserve District
Contact: (815) 877-6100; http://www.wcfpd.org/preserves/seward-bluffs
Finding the campground: Head west on US 20 from Rockford. Outside of Pecatonica, turn left on South Pecatonica Road. Turn right on Comly Road and enter the park on the right.
UTM coordinates: 16T, 304536 E, 4683073 N
About the campground: Oak, hickory, and a sprinkling of pine trees provide ample shade at this campground. Most of the camping area is open; some semiprivate sites border small ravines at the edges of the campground. The campground is perched on a 100-foot wooded bluff above Grove Creek. At the foot of the bluff, Grove Creek flows through beautiful picnicking grounds surrounded with woodland. After a picnic at the old stone bridge, consider exploring the hiking/equestrian trail that heads west alongside the creek.

The old stone bridge at Seward Bluffs Forest Preserve straddles Grove Creek.

The Rock River and Freeport Area

		Hookup Sites	Total Sites	Max RV Length	Hookups	Toilets	Showers	Drinking Water	Dump Station	Recreation	Fee	Reservations
7	Lowden State Park	80	118	45	E	F	Y	Y	Y	H	$–$$$	N
8	White Pines State Park	3	106	45	E	F	Y	Y	Y	H, F	$$	N
9	Prophetstown State Park	43	103	40	E	F	Y	Y	Y	F, L	$$–$$$	N
10	Morrison Rockwood State Park	92	92	40	E	F	Y	Y	Y	H, F, L, R, B	$$$	Y
11	Le-Aqua-Na State Park	112	177	40	E	F	Y	Y	Y	H, F, R	$$–$$$	Y
12	Apple River Canyon State Park	0	49	40	N/A	NF	N	Y	Y	H, F	$	Y

7 Lowden State Park

Location: About 25 miles southwest of Rockford
Season: Year-round
Sites: 80 sites with electrical hookups, 38 sites with no hookups; 1 cabin
Maximum length: 45 feet
Facilities: Flush toilets, water, showers, tables, grills, dump station, playground, concessions, hiking trails, picnic shelters
Fee per night: $–$$$
Management: Illinois Department of Natural Resources
Contact: (815) 732-6828; http://dnr.state.il.us/lands/Landmgt/parks/r1/lowdensp.htm
Finding the campground: From I-39 south of Rockford, head west on IL 64. Before entering Oregon and crossing the Rock River, turn right on River Road and continue to the park entrance on the left.
UTM coordinates: 16T, 307133 E, 4656029 N
About the campground: The campground, located on a bluff above the Rock River, offers sites that are well shaded and semi-open. Many campsites are close to the day-use area; look closer to the river for more secluded spots. Considered one of the most beautiful settings along the Rock River, the showpiece at this small state park is an awe-inspiring 50-foot concrete statue of a Native American overlooking the river from atop the bluff. The statue, constructed by Illinois artist Laredo Taft in 1911, is the second-largest concrete monolithic statue in the world. Lowden State Park provides a convenient place for exploring nearby places such as Lowden-Miller State Forest, Castle Rock State Park, and the towns of Oregon and Dixon.

The 50-foot concrete statue of a Native American overlooks the Rock River at Lowden State Park.

8 White Pines State Park

Location: About 30 miles southwest of Rockford
Season: Year-round
Sites: 3 sites with electrical hookups, 103 sites with no hookups
Maximum length: 45 feet
Facilities: Flush toilets, water, showers, tables, grills, dump station, playground, picnic shelters, restaurant, gift shop, cabin rentals, hiking trails
Fee per night: $$
Management: Illinois Department of Natural Resources
Contact: (815) 946-3717; http://dnr.state.il.us/lands/Landmgt/parks/r1/whitepns.htm
Finding the campground: From I-39 south of Rockford, head west on IL 64. After passing through Oregon, turn left on North Ridge Road. Turn right on White Pines Road and look for the park entrance on the right.
UTM coordinates: 16T, 295129 E, 4651543 N
About the campground: This charming 385-acre park invites visitors to explore the hilly terrain, traverse the many log footbridges over Pine and Spring Creeks, and trace the route of the creeks as they flow past moss- and vine-covered limestone cliffs. From the semi-open camping area, you can walk less than a mile for breakfast at the park's log-cabin-style lodge built by the Civilian Conservation Corps in the 1930s. Among the park's unique features are the vehicular river crossings: These fords require visitors to drive through the creek (high water sometimes closes the crossings). While hiking the park's trails, you'll encounter the southernmost natural pine forest in the Midwest.

9 Prophetstown State Park

Location: About 14 miles southwest of Sterling/Rock Falls
Season: Mid-Apr to Nov
Sites: 43 sites with electrical hookups, 60 sites with no hookups
Maximum length: 40 feet
Facilities: Flush toilets, water, showers, tables, grills, dump station, boat launch
Fee per night: $$-$$$
Management: Illinois Department of Natural Resources
Contact: (815) 537-2926; http://dnr.state.il.us/lands/Landmgt/parks/r1/prophet.htm
Finding the campground: From the Quad Cities area, take I-88 northeast to IL 78. Head south on IL 78. In Prophetstown, turn left on East Third Street and turn left again on Park Street.
UTM coordinates: 16T, 256417 E, 4617357 N
About the campground: Once the site of a Native American village, this fifty-three-acre park on the shore of the Rock River is located at the edge of the small village of Prophetstown. Stately specimens of maple, cottonwood, oak, walnut, and locust trees shade the open camping area. Some of the best campsites are located close to the river. Coon Creek wriggles through the park's flat bottomland terrain toward its rendezvous with the Rock River. Within the small downtown area of Prophetstown, keep an eye out for the series of murals depicting scenes from the town's history.

10 Morrison Rockwood State Park

Location: About 15 miles west of Rock Falls
Season: Year-round
Sites: 92 sites with electrical hookups
Maximum length: 40 feet
Facilities: Flush toilets, water, tables, grills, showers, dump station, boat ramp, concessions, restaurant, hiking and equestrian trails, boat rentals
Fee per night: $$$
Management: Illinois Department of Natural Resources
Contact: Call (815) 772-4708 for reservations; http://dnr.state.il.us/lands/Landmgt/parks/r1/morrison.htm
Finding the campground: From the Quad Cities area, take I-88 northeast to IL 78. Go north on IL 78. In Morrison, head west on US 30. Turn right on North Orange Street and turn left on Crosby Road, which leads to the park entrance.
UTM coordinates: 16T, 253873 E, 4637635 N
About the campground: One of the most popular outdoor recreation spots in northern Illinois, this well-kept park focuses on Lake Carlton, a stream-fed reservoir considered a prime fishing spot. Trails for hikers and equestrians crisscross the park's 1,164 acres of rolling terrain laden with hickory, ash, oak, and walnut trees. The thick stands of hardwoods in the camping areas create a private setting for most sites. Don't miss the covered bridge just south of the park on North Orange Street.

11 Le-Aqua-Na State Park

Location: About 15 miles northwest of Freeport and 6 miles south of the Wisconsin border
Season: Year-round
Sites: 112 sites with electrical hookups, 65 sites with no hookups; 7 wheelchair-accessible sites
Maximum length: 40 feet
Facilities: Flush toilets, water, showers, tables, grills, dump station, beach, boat launch, picnic shelters, trails, equestrian camping
Fee per night: $$-$$$
Management: Illinois Department of Natural Resources
Contact: (815) 369-4282 for reservations; http://dnr.state.il.us/lands/Landmgt/parks/r1/leaquana.htm
Finding the campground: From Freeport, head west on US 20. Turn right on Galena Road and enter Lena. In Lena, turn right on North Freedom Street (CR 7). The entrance to the park is on the left.
UTM coordinates: 16T, 267076 E, 4700403 N
About the campground: The camping areas at this 715-acre state park are situated on a wooded hill above the pleasant human-made lake that serves as the centerpiece for the park. Campsites are shaded and ample. Hikers can circumnavigate the forty-acre lake on trails that run through

rolling terrain laden with oaks, maples, walnuts, hickories, sweet gums, and stands of pine. Anglers come to launch their boats (no motors) and cast their lines from docks, lakeside benches, and the earthen dam on the west side of the lake. Bicyclists will want to head for the Jane Addams Recreation Trail 7 miles to the west.

12 Apple River Canyon State Park

Location: About 20 miles east of Galena
Season: Year-round
Sites: 49 sites with no hookups, 2 wheelchair-accessible sites
Maximum length: 40 feet
Facilities: Vault toilets, water, tables, grills, dump station, concessions, hiking trails, picnic shelters
Fee per night: $
Management: Illinois Department of Natural Resources
Contact: (815) 745-3302; reservations accepted; http://dnr.state.il.us/lands/Landmgt/parks/r1/apple.htm
Finding the campground: Heading west on US 20 from Freeport, turn right on South Canyon Park Road after passing Stockton. The camping area is on the left after crossing the Apple River.
UTM coordinates: 15T, 742333 E, 4703783 N
About the campground: This off-the-beaten-path campground offers one of the most beautiful settings in northern Illinois. The campsites are nicely spaced out; thick groves of oak and maple provide campers with plenty of shade and privacy. The park is bisected by the Apple River, which flows through a series of limestone canyons within the park. The walls of the canyons are dotted with mosses, lichens, and small bushes that grow in the crevices. Hiking trails allow visitors to catch the views from atop the limestone bluffs, explore the deep ravines, and wander alongside the Apple River.

The Mississippi River

	Hookup Sites	Total Sites	Max RV Length	Hookups	Toilets	Showers	Drinking Water	Dump Station	Recreation	Fee	Reservations
13 Blanding Landing Recreation Area	30	37	40	E	NF	Y	Y	Y	F, L	$$	Y
14 Mississippi Palisades State Park	110	241	40	E	F	Y	Y	Y	H	$$–$$$	N
15 Bulger's Hollow	0	26	35	N/A	NF	N	Y	Y	F, L	$	N
16 Thomson Causeway Recreation Area	126	131	45	E	NF	Y	Y	Y	H, F, L	$$	Y
17 Lock and Dam 13	0	5	35	N/A	NF	N	Y	N	F, L, C	$	N
18 Illiniwek Forest Preserve	59	84	40	E, W	F	Y	Y	Y	F, L, C	$$–$$$	N
19 Fisherman's Corner	51	56	50	E	F	Y	Y	Y	F	$$	Y

13 Blanding Landing Recreation Area

Location: About 13 miles south of Galena
Season: Mid-May to Nov
Sites: 30 sites with electrical hookups, 7 tenting sites with no hookups
Maximum length: 40 feet
Facilities: Vault toilets, water, tables, grills, dump station, showers, boat launch, playground, picnic shelter
Fee per night: $$
Management: U.S. Army Corps of Engineers
Contact: (815) 591-2326; www.mvr.usace.army.mil/missriver; 877-444-6777 or www.recreation.gov for reservations
Finding the campground: From Savanna, head north on IL 84. In Hanover, turn left on Dayton Avenue and continue to the right as it turns into Blanding Road. Keep straight ahead as West Blanding Road turns into South River Road at the Old Blanding Tavern. The campground entrance appears after crossing the railroad tracks.
UTM coordinates: 15T, 714148 E, 4684531 N
About the campground: This out-of-the-way campground is set within bottomland woods right on the banks of the Mississippi. The campsites are well shaded, grassy, and mostly open—many with views of the river. Light sleepers will want to camp closer to the river, away from the active train tracks. At 1.5 miles in width, this stretch of the Upper Mississippi River is like a large moving lake. Visitors launch boats here to fish and explore the many islands, the expansive wetlands, and the dense bottomland woods. Visitors also come to this area to experience the beautiful rugged terrain.

14 Mississippi Palisades State Park

Location: About 30 miles southeast of Galena
Season: Year-round
Sites: 110 sites with electrical hookups, 131 sites with no hookups
Maximum length: 40 feet
Facilities: Flush toilets, water, tables, grills, showers, dump station, camp store, hiking trails, overlooks
Fee per night: $$–$$$
Management: Illinois Department of Natural Resources
Contact: (815) 273-2731; http://dnr.state.il.us/lands/Landmgt/parks/r1/palisade.htm
Finding the campground: From the Freeport area, head west on US 20. After passing through Elizabeth, turn left on IL 84. The park appears on the left before entering Savanna.
UTM coordinates: 15T, 734258 E, 4669541 N
About the campground: The 2,500-acre Mississippi Palisades State Park is one of the sparkling jewels in the crown of the Illinois state park system. The park is chock-full of deep wooded ravines, slopes peppered with ferns and wildflowers, rocky limestone outcroppings, and high bluffs where you can enjoy some of the best views in the state. A series of overlooks in the south section of the park allow you to take in the 2-mile width of Old Man River as it snakes around dozens of islands and through backwater wetlands. While the campground is large, open, and rambling, the individual sites offer little privacy. Both shaded and unshaded sites are available.

15 Bulger's Hollow

Location: About 3 miles north of Clinton, Iowa, on the Iowa side of the Mississippi River
Season: Year-round
Sites: 26 sites with no hookups
Maximum length: 35 feet
Facilities: Vault toilets, water, tables, dump station, picnic shelter, playground, boat launch
Fee per night: $ (fees collected mid-May to mid-Sept)
Management: U.S. Army Corps of Engineers
Contact: (815) 259-3628; www.mvr.usace.army.mil/missriver
Finding the campground: From I-88 to the east, head northwest on US 30. Turn right on IL 136 and enter Iowa after crossing the Mississippi River. In Clinton, turn right on US 67. Turn right on 170th Street (Bulgers Hollow Road). The campground is at the end of the road.
UTM coordinates: 15T, 733629 E, 4646249 N
About the campground: This basic campground is situated in a remote, eye-catching spot between soaring river bluffs and the largest open-water pool on the Upper Mississippi River. Within the 3.5-mile-wide pool, large swaths of wetlands provide places for waterbirds to congregate. The campground is flat and well shaded by oak and cottonwood trees. Many sites are steps from the water. Behind the campground, patches of exposed sandstone decorate the river bluffs. The road down to the campground winds through a deep wooded ravine with more rocky outcroppings.

Bulger's Hollow sits alongside the widest point in the Upper Mississippi River.

16 Thomson Causeway Recreation Area

Location: About 12 miles northeast of Clinton, Iowa
Season: Mid Apr to Nov
Sites: 126 sites with electrical hookup, 5 tenting sites
Maximum length: 45 feet
Facilities: Vault toilets, water, tables, grills, dump station, showers, picnic areas, biking and hiking trails, river access
Fee per night: $$
Management: U.S. Army Corps of Engineers
Contact: (815) 259-2353; (877) 444-6777 or www.recreation.gov for reservations
Finding the campground: From Clinton, Iowa-Fulton, Illinois, area, head north on IL 84. In Thomson, head west on West Main Street. Turn left on Lewis Avenue and enter the park.
UTM coordinates: 15T 738849 E, 4047090 N
About the campground: Built mostly on an island in the backwater of the Mississippi River, this campground allows visitors views of the widest spot on the Upper Mississippi—3.5 miles

from shore to shore. From your campsite, watch the huge barges heading up and down the river or watch a flock of pelicans fly overhead. The backwater wetlands east of the island are rife with wildlife. This gem of a setting caters mainly to RVers who don't mind if the partially shaded campsites are closely situated. To see more expansive wetlands and a unique sand prairie, consider taking a hike or bike ride along the Great River Trail, which heads south near the guardhouse.

17 Lock and Dam 13

Location: 35 miles northeast of the Quad Cities
Season: Year-round
Sites: 5 sites with no hookups
Maximum length: 35 feet
Facilities: Vault toilets, grills, tables, picnic shelter (water available nearby at the lock and dam)
Fee per night: $
Management: U.S. Army Corps of Engineers
Contact: (815) 259-3628; www.mvr.usace.army.mil/missriver
Finding the campground: From I-88 to the east, head northwest on US 30. Turn right on IL 136 and then turn right again on IL 84 before reaching Fulton. Turn left on Lock Road. On the way out to the lock and dam, turn right on the unmarked gravel road on the right. Campsites are situated along this short gravel road.
UTM coordinates: 15T, 738136 E, 4642748 N
About the campground: This primitive campground sits alongside a stretch of backwater wetlands near a lock and dam on the Mississippi River. The sites are shaded and grassy. In the nearby wetlands, waterbirds congregate around a couple islands and the big swaths of cattails and sedge grasses. A short stroll from the campground, visitors can climb up to the small observation deck for a view of the dam and the opportunity to watch the boats pass through the locks. For some, the close proximity of IL 84 will put a dent in the peaceful atmosphere. A bicycle trail between Thomson and Fulton passes close to the campground.

18 Illiniwek Forest Preserve

Location: About 5 miles northwest of the Quad Cities
Season: Beginning of Apr to the beginning of Nov
Sites: 59 sites with water and electrical hookups, 25 sites with no hookups
Maximum length: 40 feet
Facilities: Flush toilets, grills, showers, water, tables, dump station, picnic shelter, playground, boat launch
Fee per night: $$–$$$
Management: Rock Island County Forest Preserve District
Contact: (309) 496-2620

Finding the campground: From the Quad Cities, take IL 84 north. After passing through Hampton, the park is on the left. From I-80 to the north, exit heading south on IL 84. After passing Fisherman's Corner Campground, enter the campground on the right.

UTM coordinates: 15T, 716543 E, 4604376 N

About the campground: This roadside campground overlooks Lock and Dam 14 where it spans a 0.5-mile-wide stretch of the Mississippi River. The campground is flat, open, and mostly shaded. The tent-camping sites hug the riverbank while the sites with hookups sit further back from the river. In either location, you can watch the progression of river barges moving up and down the waterway (watch for coal going upriver and grain coming down). The Great River Trail, a multiuse path than runs from the Quad Cities north to Albany, cuts through the campground.

19 Fisherman's Corner

Location: About 5 miles northwest of the Quad Cities
Season: Mid-Apr to the end of Oct
Sites: 51 sites with electrical hookups, 5 tenting sites
Maximum length: 50 feet
Facilities: Flush toilets, showers, grills, water, tables, dump station, picnic shelter, river access
Fee per night: $$
Management: U.S. Army Corps of Engineers
Contact: (815) 259-3628; www.mvr.usace.army.mil/missriver/; (877) 444-6777 or www .recreation.gov for reservations
Finding the campground: From the Quad Cities, take IL 84 north. After passing Hampton and the Illiniwek Forest Preserve, the park is on the left. From I-80 to the north, exit heading south on IL 84. Before passing through Hampton, enter the campground on the right.
UTM coordinates: 15T, 717558 E, 4605031 N
About the campground: This roadside campground offers prime views of Lock and Dam 14 and a swath of Mississippi River wetlands. The tightly clustered, side-by-side configuration of the sites is better suited to RV campers. Some sites are against the water; many are not. A couple of miles upstream is the village of Rapid City, named for the rapids that once existed on this section of the river. Before the rapids were removed with dynamite, riverboats had to unload cargo onto a train, transport it north, and then load it on another boat upstream.

The Illinois River and the Hennepin Canal

		Hookup Sites	Total Sites	Max RV Length	Hookups	Toilets	Showers	Drinking Water	Dump Station	Recreation	Fee	Reservations
20	Hennepin Canal Lock 23	0	2	N/A	N/A	NF	N	N	N	H, C, L	$	N
21	Hennepin Canal Lock 22	0	4	N/A	N/A	NF	N	Y	N	H, C, R, L	$	N
22	Hennepin Canal Lock 21	0	6	N/A	N/A	NF	N	Y	N	H, C, R, L	$	N
23	Hennepin Canal Lock 17	0	6	N/A	N/A	NF	N	N	N	H, C, R, L	$	N
24	Hennepin Canal Lock 11	0	4	N/A	N/A	NF	N	N	N	H, C, R, L	$	N
25	Green River State Wildlife Area	0	10	35	N/A	NF	N	Y	Y	H, R	$	N
26	Starved Rock State Park	133	133	45	E	F	Y	Y	Y	H, F, L	$$$	Y
27	I&M Canal Trail: Buffalo Rock State Park	0	3	N/A	N/A	N/A	N	N	N	H, C, F	$	N

20 Hennepin Canal Lock 23

Location: About 30 miles east of the Quad Cities
Season: Year-round
Sites: 2 walk-in sites
Maximum length: N/A
Facilities: Vault toilets, tables, grills, canal lock, multiuse trail, no drinking water available
Fee per night: $
Management: Illinois Department of Natural Resources
Contact: (815) 454-2328; http://dnr.state.il.us/lands/landmgt/parks/r1/hennpin.htm
Finding the campground: From I-80 in Annawan, exit north on IL 78. After crossing the canal, turn left on CR1900 North. Continue ahead as CR1900 North becomes CR1920 North. Look for the parking area on the right.
UTM coordinates: 16T, 252240 E, 4590322 N
About the campground: This postage-stamp-sized rustic camping area sits beside the Hennepin Canal and the accompanying trail, which runs for 62 miles between the Illinois and the Rock Rivers. The camping area is grassy and open. A short pedestrian bridge spans the canal; cottonwood trees grow on the nearby banks. Engineering buffs will enjoy the still-intact mechanical devices on the locks, as well as the aqueduct just 2.5 miles east along the canal trail.

Many of the locks on the Hennepin Canal, including Lock 23, still have the original machinery intact.

21 Hennepin Canal Lock 22

Location: About 35 miles east of the Quad Cities
Season: Year-round
Sites: 4 walk-in sites
Maximum length: N/A
Facilities: Vault toilets, water, tables, multiuse trail, grills, picnic area, canal lock, boat launch
Fee per night: $
Management: Illinois Department of Natural Resources
Contact: (815) 454-2328; http://dnr.state.il.us/lands/landmgt/parks/r1/hennpin.htm
Finding the campground: From I-80 in Annawan, exit south on IL 78. Turn left on US 6. After passing through Mineral, turn left on 1550 Avenue North. Turn right on 300 East Street. The camping area is on the left.
UTM coordinates: 16T, 266011 E, 4586848 N
About the campground: This is one of a handful of quiet camping spots alongside the Hennepin Canal Trail, which runs for 62 miles between the Illinois and the Rock Rivers. The two camping areas, on the either side of the canal just west of the lock, are open and grassy with ample shade. Corn plants dominate the surrounding landscape. The locks still have wooden gates intact, as well as the gears, pulleys, and the counterweights that lifted the small drawbridge over the canal. The Feeder Basin, where the Feeder Canal meets the Main Canal, is less than 1 mile east along the canal. Canoeists like to put in at Lock 22 because they can paddle nearly 10 miles west to Lock 23 with no portages.

22 Hennepin Canal Lock 21

Location: 45 miles west of the Quad Cities
Season: Year-round
Sites: 6 sites with no hookups, 6 sites for equestrian camping
Maximum length: N/A
Facilities: Vault toilets, water, grills, tables, boat launch, canal locks, multiuse trail, picnic shelter
Fee per night: $
Management: Illinois Department of Natural Resources
Contact: (815) 454-2328; http://dnr.state.il.us/lands/landmgt/parks/r1/hennpin.htm
Finding the campground: About 45 miles west of the Quad Cities along I-80, exit south on IL 40. Turn left on US 34/6. After crossing the canal several miles ahead, look for the entrance to the camping/picnic area on the right.
UTM coordinates: 16T, 281567 E, 4582293 N
About the campground: A few of these open, grassy campsites offer some degree of privacy. Some sites are situated on the edge of the canal, and all are shaded by stately cottonwoods. The canal, which runs for 62 miles between the Illinois and the Rock Rivers, widens at this location. The lines of concrete blocks near the campsites are the remains of a boat repair yard that once stood on the property. A few more historical attractions related to the canal are near Wyanet, 1 mile to the east.

23 Hennepin Canal Lock 17

Location: 45 miles west of the Quad Cities
Season: Year-round
Sites: 6 tenting sites
Maximum length: N/A
Facilities: Vault toilets, grills, tables, multiuse trail, no drinking water available
Fee per night: $
Management: Illinois Department of Natural Resources
Contact: (815) 454-2328; http://dnr.state.il.us/lands/landmgt/parks/r1/hennpin.htm
Finding the campground: About 45 miles west of the Quad Cites along I-80, exit south on IL 40. Turn left on US 34/6. In Wyanet, turn right on Wyanet-Walnut Road (CR 8). Turn left on West Canal Street (CR 1410 North). Turn right on CR 1550 East. From the east on I-80, exit south at IL 26. In Princeton, turn left on the US 6/34. Before Wyanet, turn left on CR 1600 East. Turn right on CR 1400 North. Turn left on CR 1550 East.
UTM coordinates: 16T, 286036E, 4579906 N
About the campground: This no-frills, roadside camping spot sits within the most historically interesting section of the Hennepin Canal, which runs for 62 miles between the Illinois and the Rock Rivers. The camping area is a grassy lawn at the foot of a vine-covered train trestle bridge. Visitors can climb up on the bridge for a better view of the canal and the surrounding landscape. Another old bridge at this lock was built on a system of rollers so that it could be moved out of the way for canal boats. In either direction along the trail, you'll encounter aqueducts and a handful of locks, many with the original mechanical devices still intact.

24 Hennepin Canal Lock 11

Location: About 50 miles west of the Quad Cities
Season: Year-round
Sites: 4 tenting sites
Maximum length: N/A
Facilities: Vault toilets, tables, grills, picnic shelter, multiuse trail, no drinking water available
Fee per night: $
Management: Illinois Department of Natural Resources
Contact: (815) 454-2328; http://dnr.state.il.us/lands/landmgt/parks/r1/hennpin.htm
Finding the campground: From I-80 north of Princeton, exit south on IL 26. As IL 26 turns left, keep straight ahead on South Main Street, which turns into Tiskilwa Bottom Road. Stay right on Princeton-Tiskilwa Road (CR 1250 North). Just after crossing the canal, you'll see the camping area on the left.
UTM coordinates: 16T, 289741 E, 4576561 N
About the campground: An old scenic trestle bridge overlooks this small roadside camping spot. The bridge spans the Hennepin Canal and its multiuse trail alongside it; both run for 62 miles between the Illinois and the Rock Rivers. The small camping area is open, grassy, and shaded by sycamores and firs. A small farm and some rolling hills border this little park. A moderate amount of traffic runs by the park on Princeton-Tiskilwa Road.

25 Green River State Wildlife Area

Location: 55 miles southwest of Rockford
Season: Year-round
Sites: 10 sites with no hookups
Maximum length: 35 feet
Facilities: Vault toilets, grills, water, tables, dump station, picnic shelter, hiking and equestrian trails
Fee per night: $
Management: Illinois Department of Natural Resources
Contact: (815) 379-2324; http://dnr.state.il.us/lands/landmgt/parks/r1/green.htm
Finding the campground: From I-88 near Dixon, head south on IL 26. After 13 miles, turn right on Maytown Road. Follow signs to the check station. The camping area is across the road from the check station.
UTM coordinates: 16T, 290426 E, 4611779 N
About the campground: This primitive, out-of-the-way campground is situated in an open grassy area sprinkled with large oak trees. In May, when the prairie flowers bloom, the nearby grassland is blanketed with color. The campground is located close to the hunter's check station and one of the park's maintenance barns. The terrain of the 2,500-acre park is varied: in addition to the prairie, there are large sections containing wetlands and rolling woodland.

26 Starved Rock State Park

Location: 90 miles southwest of Chicago
Season: Year-round
Sites: 133 sites with electrical hookups, 7 wheelchair-accessible sites
Maximum length: 45 feet
Facilities: Flush toilets, grills, showers, water, tables, dump station, picnic shelter, playground, hiking trails, park lodge, cabins, visitor center, campground store
Fee per night: $$$
Management: Illinois Department of Natural Resources
Contact: (815) 667-4726; http://dnr.state.il.us/lands/landmgt/parks/i&m/east/starve/park .htm; reservations accepted
Finding the campground: From I-80, take exit 81 south into Utica on IL 178. Cross the Illinois River and pass the main entrance to the park. Then turn left on IL 71. Turn right on East 950th Road and follow signs for the campground.
UTM coordinates: 16T, 334327 E, 4574077 N
About the campground: Many of the campsites at Illinois' most popular state park are perched on the upper edge of a ravine; some border nearby prairie and savanna. Generally, the sites are flat, partially shaded, and open; many are fairly private with ample space between them. Be sure to check out the park's spectacular trails: They run along the shore of the Illinois River, over the soaring river bluffs, and through the dramatic sandstone canyons. It's a busy park, so expect a bustling atmosphere unless you arrive during the week or the off-season.

Fantastic rock formations abound at Starved Rock State Park.

27 I&M Canal Trail: Buffalo Rock State Park

Location: 40 miles west of Joliet
Season: Year-round
Sites: 3 hike-in sites spread out along the I&M Canal between Buffalo Rock State Park and Utica
Maximum length: N/A
Facilities: Fire rings, picnic shelter and stone fireplace at the westernmost site, drinking water available at Buffalo Rock State Park
Fee per night: $ (pay at Buffalo Rock State Park)
Management: Illinois Department of Natural Resources
Contact: (815) 942-0796; http://dnr.state.il.us/lands/landmgt/parks/i&m/main.htm
Finding the campground: From I-80 to the north, take exit 90 south toward Ottawa. Follow IL 23 south. Turn right on US 6, then turn left on Boyce Memorial Drive. After 1 mile, veer right onto Ottawa Avenue, which eventually becomes North 27th Road (Dee Bennett Road). Just after passing the entrance to Buffalo Rock State Park on the left, park in the I&M Canal Trail parking area on the right. Heading west from the parking area along the I&M Canal Trail, the campsites appear in roughly quarter-mile increments.
UTM coordinates: (for parking area) 16T, 339543 E, 4576859 N
About the campground: These three hike-in camping areas are located in scenic spots on the shore of a small lake and alongside a stretch of Illinois River backwater. To the north, beyond a sprawling wetland laden with cattails, you'll catch glimpses of exposed sandstone at the top of the wooded river bluffs. The two sites closest to the parking area (sites A and B) have room for a couple of tents, whereas the site farthest west (site C) has room for a half-dozen tents. This site also contains a picnic shelter and a fireplace. The list of local attractions is impressive: Starved Rock, Matthiessen, and Buffalo Rock State Parks. Very close on Dee Bennett Road is the Illinois Waterway Visitor Center at Starved Rock Lock and Dam. A platform on the second floor of the visitor center provides a great view of barges as they enter and leave the 600-foot-long lock.

Chicagoland

Like so much of Illinois, the landscape in the Chicago region is the legacy of the glaciers that covered the area. They created the local rivers—the Fox, the Des Plaines, the DuPage, the Kankakee, and the Illinois—and they steamrolled the area making it often as flat as the surface of Lake Michigan. While the surface is mostly level, topographical exceptions abound—most notably in the hills that swell in McHenry County near the Wisconsin border and the river bluffs and canyons that developed on the shore of the Kankakee and Illinois Rivers.

Despite its reputation as a place where people focus on work and little else, the Chicago area contains many places to swim, fish, hike, and bicycle. Dozens of attractive forest preserves containing stocked lakes attract boaters and anglers. Connecting many of these forest preserves is the best network of rail trails in the state. Visitors to the area come for charming suburban communities, a growing constellation of local casinos, and, of course, enough shopping options to make your head spin. And it's not as unusual as you might think for people to camp outside the city and make daytrips into Chicago to see the museums, lounge on the beaches, and explore the lively and engaging neighborhoods that lie at the heart of the city.

While the prospect of camping in Chicagoland may sound unappealing to some, for others, particularly those whose jobs and other responsibilities keep them on a short leash geographically, spending a quick night or two in the woods can be wonderfully rejuvenating. Fortunately, a variety of good campgrounds can be found in the region.

While the large local parks offer plenty to do and see, you may want to think again if you're inclined toward tranquility. At state parks such as Illinois Beach, Chain O' Lakes, and Kankakee River, campgrounds fill up fast on summer weekends. If you're looking for a quieter atmosphere, consider visiting midweek or, even better, during the off-season. You could also head toward one of the many smaller forest preserves. Marengo Ridge Conservation Area in McHenry County and McKinley Woods Forest Preserve in Will County are just a couple of smaller parks that will likely provide a more peaceful atmosphere. If you're interested in a truly remote camping experience in the region, consider one of the hike-in camping options along the I&M Canal Trail as it runs between Joliet and LaSalle.

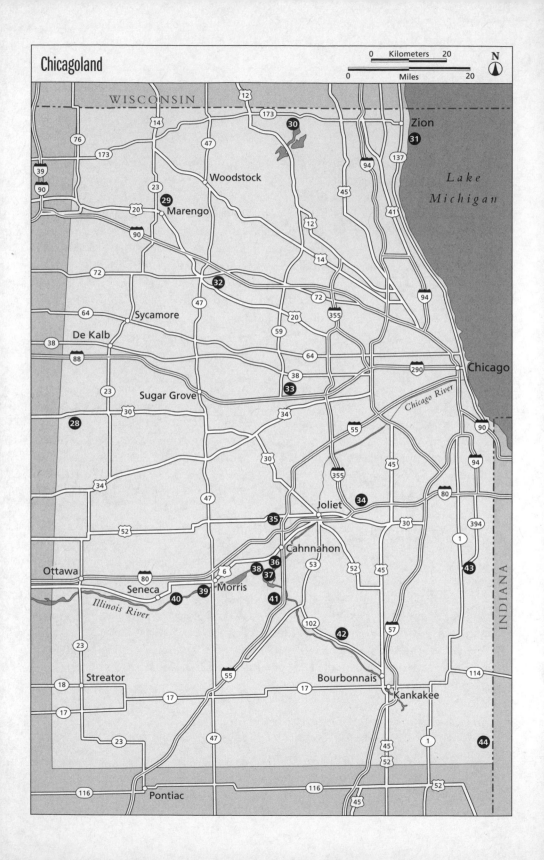

Chicagoland

		Hookup Sites	Total Sites	Max RV Length	Hookups	Toilets	Showers	Drinking Water	Dump Station	Recreation	Fee	Reservations
28	Shabbona Lake State Park	150	150	45	E	F	Y	Y	Y	B, H, F, L	$$$	Y
29	Marengo Ridge Conservation Area	2	49	40	E	F	Y	Y	Y	H, F	$-$$$	Y
30	Chain O' Lakes State Park	151	238	50	E	F	Y	Y	Y	B, C, H, F, L, R	$$-$$$	Y
31	Illinois Beach State Park	244	244	45	E	F	Y	Y	Y	C, H, S	$$$	Y
32	Burnidge Forest Preserve	48	63	45	E	NF	N	Y	Y	H, F, R	$$-$$$	N
33	Blackwell Forest Preserve	35	60	40	E	F	Y	Y	Y	B, H, F, L, C	$$-$$$	Y
34	Messenger Woods Forest Preserve	0	4	N/A	N/A	NF	N	Y	N	H, F	$$-$$$	Y
35	Hammel Woods Forest Preserve	0	6	N/A	N/A	NF	N	Y	N	H, F	$$-$$$	Y
36	Channahon State Park	0	20	N/A	N/A	NF	N	Y	N	C, H, F	$	N
37	McKinley Woods Forest Preserve	0	4	N/A	N/A	NF	N	Y	N	C, H, F	$$-$$$	N
38	I&M Canal Trail: Channahon	0	2	N/A	N/A	NF	N	Y	N	C, H, F	$	N
39	Gebhard Woods State Park	0	10	N/A	N/A	NF	N	Y	N	C, H, F	$	N
40	I&M Canal Trail: Aux Sable Aqueduct to Seneca	0	4	N/A	N/A	NF	N	N	N	C, H, F	$	N
41	Des Plaines Fish and Wildlife Area	0	22	35	N/A	NF	N	Y	N	H, F, L	$	N
42	Kankakee River State Park	219	260	45	E	F	Y	Y	Y	C, H, F, L, S, R	$$-$$$	Y
43	Goodenow Grove Nature Preserve	0	15	35	N/A	NF	N	Y	N	H	$$-$$$	Y
44	Willow Slough Fish and Wildlife Area	0	75	40	N/A	F	Y	Y	Y	B, H, F, L	$$	N

28 Shabbona Lake State Park

Location: 65 miles west of Chicago
Season: Year-round
Sites: 150 sites with electrical hookups, 2 cabins; wheelchair-accessible sites available
Maximum length: 45 feet
Facilities: Flush toilets, grills, showers, water, tables, dump station, picnic shelter, boat launch, boat rental, bait and tackle shop, playground, camp store, children's fishing pond, hiking trails, restaurant
Fee per night: $$$
Management: Illinois Department of Natural Resources
Contact: (815) 824-2565 or (815) 824-2106; http://dnr.state.il.us/lands/landmgt/parks/r1/shabbona.htm; reservations accepted
Finding the campground: From Chicago, take I-290 west to I-88. Follow I-88 west to the Sugar Grove exit. From the Sugar Grove exit, take US 30 west for 25 miles. At Indian Road turn left, and then turn right on Preserve Road. The entrance to the park is on the left.
UTM coordinates: 16T, 344471 E, 4623609 N

About the campground: While a few of the campsites offer great views of Shabbona Lake from a small grassy hilltop above the lake, most of the sites are tucked away in a pleasing wooded environment further from the lake. Trees and shrubs provide plenty of shade, as well as a buffer between the sites. During the warmer months, the park brings in a steady stream of anglers, campers, and picnickers. The rest of year, the park is surprisingly quiet. For a human-made artifact, Shabbona Lake is strikingly beautiful and varied. While hiking around the lake, you'll encounter grasslands, hills, streams, marshes, dense woodlands, and ponds.

29 Marengo Ridge Conservation Area

Location: About 25 miles east of Rockford
Season: Beginning of May to the end of Oct
Sites: 18 sites with no hookups, 2 sites with electrical hookups, 29 tent camping sites, 3 wheelchair-accessible sites
Maximum length: 40 feet
Facilities: Flush toilets, showers, grills, water, tables, dump station, picnic shelter, hiking trails, playgrounds
Fee per night: $–$$$
Management: McHenry County Conservation District
Contact: (815) 338-6223; www.mccdistrict.org/web/re-camping.htm; reservations accepted
Finding the campground: Take I-90 northwest of Chicago. Head north on US 20 after passing through Elgin. In Marengo, turn right on IL 23. The park entrance is on the right.
UTM coordinates: 16T, 367441 E, 4682352 N
About the campground: This wonderfully wooded landscape provides visitors with an unusually isolated atmosphere. The hilly terrain is crisscrossed with intermittent streams and blanketed with dense groves of oak, hickory, and conifers. The campsites are wooded and well spaced. Some of the tenting sites require a short walk from the parking spots. Visitors will find a network of hiking trails, a small fishing pond, and a short trail leading to an overlook of nearby farmland.

30 Chain O' Lakes State Park

Location: 55 miles northwest of Chicago
Season: Mid-Dec to the beginning of Nov
Sites: 151 sites with electrical hookups, 87 sites with no hookups, 3 rental cabins; wheelchair-accessible sites available
Maximum length: 50 feet
Facilities: Flush toilets, grills, showers, water, tables, dump station, picnic shelters, boat launch, concessionaire, hiking trails, fishing docks, playgrounds, horse rental, equestrian trails
Fee per night: $$–$$$

The hiking trail at Chain O' Lakes State Park meets up with a stretch of the Fox River.

Management: Illinois Department of Natural Resources
Contact: (847) 587-5512; http://dnr.state.il.us/lands/landmgt/parks/r2/chaino.htm; reservations accepted
Finding the campground: From Chicago, take I-94 north to IL 173 (Rosecrans Road). Head west on IL 173. After about 12 miles, turn left on Wilmot Road. The entrance is on the left.
UTM coordinates: 10T, 402000 E, 4700270 N
About the campground: As the largest state park in northern Illinois, Chain O' Lakes offers plenty of scenic vistas: expansive wetlands, gently rolling prairies, pleasant wooded areas, and a peaceful stretch of the Fox River. The campgrounds, located at the southern tip of the park, are densely wooded with opportunities for camping in open grassy areas. Some of the campsites are on the shore of Turner Lake, and many patches of wetland are nearby. Given the number of attractions at the park, it's no surprise that it draws crowds—particularly boaters. Despite the busy atmosphere in the summer months, tranquil hiking is readily found once you get away from the boat launch and the picnic areas.

31 Illinois Beach State Park

Location: 50 miles north of Chicago
Season: Year-round
Sites: 244 sites with electrical hookups; wheelchair-accessible sites available
Maximum length: 45 feet
Facilities: Flush toilets, showers, grills, water, tables, dump station, picnic shelter, Lake Michigan beach, concessionaire, hiking and cycling trails, hotel, marina, beach house, blacktop campsite pads, playgrounds
Fee per night: $$$
Management: Illinois Department of Natural Resources
Contact: (847) 662-4811; http://dnr.state.il.us/lands/landmgt/parks/r2/ilbeach.htm; reservations accepted
Finding the campground: Follow I-94 north from Chicago. Exit at Grand Avenue (IL 132) and go east. Turn left on Green Bay Road (IL 131) and then turn right on Wadsworth Road. Follow Wadsworth Road for 3 miles into the park and then follow signs to the campground. If you're using public transportation, take the Union Pacific/North Metro Line from Chicago to Zion. (From the Zion station, the campground is just a couple of miles away.) Head south on the path that runs on the west side of the train tracks. Turn left on Twenty-ninth Street and then continue straight on the paved path as the road turns left. Follow the path to the main beach and the campground.
UTM coordinates: 16T, 433495 E, 4697888 N
About the campground: More than sixty of the sites within this large, well-loved campground are within 200 feet of the wide sandy beach. The campground is flat with stands of oak trees offering ample shade and snatches of privacy. The park's many trails provide a break from the busy atmosphere at the main beach, the picnic area, and the campground. The nearby power plants remind you that you're still in Chicagoland. Also, no big dunes at this beach: Prevailing winds push the dunes to the south and eastern shore of the lake.

32 Burnidge Forest Preserve

Location: 40 miles northwest of downtown Chicago
Season: Beginning of May to end of Oct
Sites: 48 sites with electrical hookups,15 tent camping sites
Maximum length: 45 feet
Facilities: Vault toilets, grills, water, tables, dump station, picnic shelter, concrete pads, hiking trails
Fee per night: $$-$$$
Management: Kane County Forest Preserve District
Contact: (630) 232-5980; www.kaneforest.com/findPreserve.aspx
Finding the campground: Going west on I-90 from Chicago, head south on North Randall Road. Turn right on Big Timber Road. Enter the campground on the left and follow signs to the campground.
UTM coordinates: 16T, 387509 E, 4658199 N
About the campground: The compact camping area is fringed with attractive prairie and patches of woodland. It also sits beside a big red barn. The campground is open and offers a good amount

of shade. Not far from the main campground, the forest preserve offers a collection of secluded tent camping sites in a wooded setting. Stocked fishing ponds invite anglers to cast a line. The forest preserve hosts an impressive collection of hiking trails, as well as a small climbing wall near the main campground.

33 Blackwell Forest Preserve

Location: About 5 miles north of Naperville
Season: Open only weekends and holidays from the beginning of June to the end of Sept
Sites: 35 sites with electrical hookups, 25 sites with no hookups
Maximum length: 40 feet
Facilities: Flush toilets, water, tables, grills, showers, dump station, boat rental, hiking and biking trails, archery range
Fee per night: $$–$$$
Management: DuPage County Forest Preserve
Contact: (630) 933-7248; reservations accepted; www.dupageforest.com/Recreation/Activities AndFacilities/Camping.html

A view from atop Mount Hoy at Blackwell Forest Preserve.

Finding the campground: From I-88 near Warrenville, head north on Winfield Road. Less than 2 miles ahead, turn left on Butterfield Road (IL 56). The entrance to the park is on the right.
UTM coordinates: 16T, 402563 E, 4632275 N
About the campground: Shaded by walnut and oak trees, the campground sits on rolling terrain at the edge of Silver Lake. Some campsites overlook the small lake, where visitors can fish and rent boats. Beyond the campground, a top-notch trail system runs through woods, savanna, and a large marsh to the north. Catch the views from the second-highest point in DuPage County atop Mount Hoy (yes, it's a former landfill), located across Silver Lake from the campground.

34 Messenger Woods Forest Preserve

Location: 10 miles northeast of Joliet
Season: Year-round
Sites: 4 walk-in sites with no hookups
Maximum length: N/A
Facilities: Vault toilets, water, grills, tables, picnic shelter, hiking trails
Fee per night: $$–$$$
Management: Will County Forest Preserve District
Contact: (815) 727-8700; www.fpdwc.org/messenger.cfm; reservations accepted
Finding the campground: From I-355 near Lockport, exit east on IL 7. Turn right on South Cedar Road. Turn left on West Bruce Road. The entrance to the park is on the left.
UTM coordinates: 16T, 420618 E, 4602919 N
About the campground: This small campground is located in an open area at the edge of a dense stand of woods. Spring Creek, a short walk from the campground, has cut steep ravines through the hilly woodland. Hiking trails lead through groves of oak and maple bottomlands.

35 Hammel Woods Forest Preserve

Location: 7 miles west of Joliet
Season: Year-round
Sites: 6 walk-in sites
Maximum length: N/A
Facilities: Vault toilets, water, grills, tables, picnic shelter, paved bike trail, canoe launch
Fee per night: $$–$$$
Management: Will County Forest Preserve District
Contact: (815) 727-8700; www.fpdwc.org/hammel.cfm; reservations accepted
Finding the campground: On I-55 west of Joliet, head west on US 52 (exit 253). Immediately turn right on Northwest Frontage Road. Turn left on West Black Road. Enter the DuPage River Access Area on the left.
UTM coordinates: 16T, 400807 E, 4598660 N
About the campground: Hammel Woods features trails, woods, and a stretch of river that meanders around several islands. The walk-in campsites are close to the DuPage River. The seven-acre dog

park and the nearby traffic of I-55 lend the park a bustling atmosphere. The paved DuPage River Trail and other hiking trails allow visitors to explore the park's attractive woods and the river. Canoeists can put it at Hammel Woods and paddle for two hours to McKinley Woods in Channahon.

36 Channahon State Park

Location: 12 mile southwest of Joliet
Season: Year-round
Sites: 20 walk-in sites
Maximum length: N/A
Facilities: Vault toilets, grills, water, tables, multiuse trail
Fee per night: $
Management: Illinois Department of Natural Resources
Contact: (815) 467-4271; http://dnr.state.il.us/lands/landmgt/parks/i&m/east/channaho/park.htm
Finding the campground: From Chicago, take I-55 south of I-80. Exit I-55 west on US 6. In Channahon, turn left on South Canal Street. The entrance to the park is on the right.
UTM coordinates: 16T, 397352 E, 4586318 N

Channahon State Park contains one of the only locktender's houses left on the I&M Canal.

About the campground: This small park is a favorite local spot to pick up the 61-mile I&M Canal Trail on its way from Joliet to LaSalle. In addition to hosting the trail, the park features an attractive picnic area and a well-shaded open campground for tent camping. The campground adjoins a residential neighborhood in the town of Channahon. Along the trail, you can explore the locktender's house and a couple of locks before embarking on one of the best sections of the canal trail: As the trail heads west, it follows a thin sliver of land between the Des Plaines River and the I&M Canal.

37 McKinley Woods Forest Preserve

Location: About 18 miles southwest of Joliet
Season: Year-round
Sites: 4 walk-in sites
Maximum length: N/A
Facilities: Vault toilets, grills, water, tables, picnic shelter, hiking trails, multiuse trail
Fee per night: $$–$$$
Management: Will County Forest Preserve
Contact: (815) 727-8700; www.fpdwc.org/mckinley.cfm
Finding the campground: From Chicago, take I-55 south of I-80 to exit 248. From this exit, head southwest on US 6. After passing through Channahon, turn left on McKinley Woods Road and proceed for 2.5 miles. Park at the Frederick's Grove picnic area at the end of the road.
UTM coordinates: 16T, 396224 E, 4582025 N
About the campground: Just before the Des Plaines River meets the Kankakee River to become the Illinois River, the Des Plaines arcs around a series of steep bluffs and plunging ravines. The inside of the arc is tipped by McKinley Woods, where you'll find 473 acres of dramatic slopes, thick with oak and hickory, overlooking the Des Plaines River and the I&M Canal. The quiet camping area at McKinley Woods sits at the foot of the bluff; it's flat and grassy, with little shade. The campground is a short walk from a stretch of the canal where it becomes a large wetland. The wooded bluffs, the close proximity to the Des Plaines and the Illinois Rivers, and the historical attractions make this a favorite stretch of the I&M Canal Trail.

38 I&M Canal Trail: Channahon

Location: About 18 miles southwest of Joliet
Season: Year-round
Sites: 2 hike-in sites
Maximum length: N/A
Facilities: Vault toilets, fire ring, shelter, water at McKinley Woods Forest Preserve
Fee per night: $ (pay at Channahon State Park)
Management: Illinois Department of Natural Resources
Contact: (815) 467-4271; http://dnr.state.il.us/lands/landmgt/parks/i&m/main.htm
Finding the campground: Campers must park overnight at Channahon State Park and hike 3.5 miles along the I&M Canal Trail to the campsite. From Chicago, take I-55 south of I-80. Exit I-55

west on US 6. In Channahon, turn left on South Canal Street. The entrance to the park is on the right. At the locktender's house, turn left on the trail and proceed for 3.5 miles on foot or bicycle. Just after passing the river-viewing platform and McKinley Woods pedestrian bridge, look for the trail leading left to the campsites along the Illinois River.

UTM coordinates: 16T, 395982 E, 4582023 N

About the campground: One of the best hike-in camping options along the 61-mile-long I&M Canal Trail sits on a narrow strip of land between the Des Plaines River and a spot where the canal widens to become a wetland. Above the canal are the steep wooded bluffs of McKinley Woods, a county park that also offers camping. Dense stands of maple trees provide shade for the grassy camping area that sits against the shore of the river. After exploring the rugged terrain at McKinley Woods, head west on the I&M Canal Trail to see the Dresden Lock and Dam.

39 Gebhard Woods State Park

Location: 25 miles southwest of Joliet
Season: Year-round
Sites: 10 hike-in sites
Maximum length: N/A
Facilities: Vault toilets, water, tables, picnic shelter, fire rings
Fee per night: $
Management: Illinois Department of Natural Resources
Contact: (815) 942-0796; http://dnr.state.il.us/lands/landmgt/parks/i&m/east/gebhard/park.htm
Finding the campground: From I-80, head south into Morris on IL 47. Turn right on West Jefferson Street, which soon becomes Freemont Street. After turning left on Ottawa Street, the entrance to the park is on the left.
UTM coordinates: 16T, 379768 E, 4579316 N
About the campground: Nettle Creek winds around this open, grassy tenting campground. The camping area, which requires a one-third-mile hike from the parking lot, is shaded by mature oaks. Gebhard Woods is a small but active park that abuts residential areas in the town of Morris. The south side of the park is bordered by the 61-mile-long I&M Canal Trail. The trail west of the Gebhard Woods has a gloriously remote ambience.

40 I&M Canal Trail: Aux Sable Aqueduct to Seneca

Location: About 25 miles southwest of Joliet
Season: Year-round
Sites: 4 sites spread out along the I&M Canal Trail between Aux Sable Aqueduct to the east and Seneca to the west: one is a roadside camping spot, and the other three are hike- or bike-in sites
Maximum length: N/A
Facilities: Fire rings, vault toilets (water only at the Aux Sable Aqueduct)
Fee per night: $ (pay at Channahon State Park for camping at Aux Sable Aqueduct; pay at Gebhard Woods State Park for camping at the other three sites)

Management: Illinois Department of Natural Resources

Contact: (815) 942-0796; http://dnr.state.il.us/lands/landmgt/parks/i&m/main.htm

Finding the campground: These four campsites are spread out along 16 miles of the I&M Canal Trail between the Aux Sable Aqueduct and the town of Seneca. To reach the Aux Sable Aqueduct camping area from Chicago, take I-55 south of I-80 to exit 248. From this exit, head southwest on US 6. Eight miles ahead turn left on South Tabler Road. Turn right on Cemetery Road. The other three campsites are accessible from Gebhard Woods State Park and require campers to hike (or bike) anywhere from 1.5 to 8 miles. To reach Gebhard Woods from I-80, head south into Morris on IL 47. Turn right on West Jefferson Street, which soon becomes Freemont Street. After turning left on Ottawa Street, the entrance to the park is on the left. One site is 3.5 miles east of Gebhard Woods on the trail, another is 2.5 miles west of Gebhard Woods, and one is about 8 miles west of Gebhard Woods.

UTM coordinates: (Aux Sable Aqueduct) 16T, 388552 E, 4583295 N

About the campground: The Aux Sable camping area is within a grassy roadside park next to a former locktender's house along the Illinois & Michigan Canal. The locktender had to be available day or night to raise and lower the boats in the canal. Visitors can still marvel at the engineering feat of routing the canal over Aux Sable Creek. All the hike-in camping spots are wooded and isolated. The first one west of Aux Sable Aqueduct is situated near a large wetland. The next one heading west is located near a stream that empties into the Illinois River. The final campsite, located near Seneca, sits within a dense woodland fringed by prairie.

41 Des Plaines Fish and Wildlife Area

Location: 15 miles southwest of Joliet

Season: Mid-Apr to mid-Oct

Sites: 22 sites with no hookups

Maximum length: 35 feet

Facilities: Vault toilets, grills, water, tables, picnic area, playground, boat launch, equestrian trails, archery range, trap shooting range

Fee per night: $

Management: Illinois Department of Natural Resources

Contact: (815) 423-5326; http://dnr.state.il.us/lands/landmgt/parks/i&m/east/desplain/park.htm

Finding the campground: From Chicago, take I-55 south. South of I-80, head west on North River Road (exit 241). Cross the railroad tracks and then turn left on the park road. The camping area is on the left.

UTM coordinates: 16T, 398939 E, 4579012 N

About the campground: The bottomland terrain of this park contains plenty of agricultural fields, wetland, ponds, and backwater. Some campsites sit very close to the backwater of the Kankakee River. Thick oak woods offer plenty of shade, and a couple of close-by ponds add to the atmosphere. The campground lies out of earshot of I-55, but nearby railroad tracks host frequent trains. In the vicinity, explore miles of trails at Midewin National Tallgrass Prairie and Goose Lake Prairie State Park.

Rock Creek before it empties into the Kankakee River.

42 Kankakee River State Park

Location: 25 miles south of Joliet

Season: Year-round

Sites: 219 sites with electrical hookups, 41 sites with no hookups, 2 rental cabins

Maximum length: 45 feet

Facilities: Flush toilets, showers, grills, water, tables, dump station, picnic shelters, hiking and biking trails, playgrounds, boat launch, horse rentals, equestrian trails, concessionaire

Fee per night: $$–$$$

Management: Illinois Department of Natural Resources

Contact: (815) 933 1383; http://dnr.state.il.us/lands/landmgt/parks/r2/kankakee.htm; reservations accepted

Finding the campground: From Chicago, take I-94 south to I-57. At exit 315 north of Kankakee, leave I-57 and head south on IL 50. Quickly turn right on Armour Road. Turn right on IL 102 and continue for 5 miles. One campground is south of the visitor center and one is to the north along IL 102.

UTM coordinates: (visitor center) 16T, 417903 E, 4561576 N

About the campground: Both campgrounds at this park are located on the tops of bluffs above the Kankakee River. Most sites are clustered together in fairly tight arrangements. The Potawatomi Campground offers shaded sites closer to the river and further from IL 102. This 11-mile-long state park straddles both sides of the Kankakee River. The river's wooded shores and unpolluted water bring in the boaters and the anglers. The star attractions of the park are the craggy cliffs and vertical walls of Rock Creek Canyon as it gently curves toward the Kankakee River. One must-do for visitors is a hike along Rock Creek to see a frothy waterfall at the end of the trail.

43 Goodenow Grove Nature Preserve

Location: 35 miles south of downtown Chicago
Season: Year-round
Sites: 15 sites with no hookups
Maximum length: 35 feet
Facilities: Vault toilets, water, grills, tables, picnic shelters, nature center, sledding hill, ice-skating pond
Fee per night: $$–$$$
Management: Will County Forest Preserve District
Contact: (815) 727-8700; www.fpdwc.org/goodenow.cfm; reservations accepted
Finding the campground: From Chicago, take I-94 south to I-80. At I-80, continue south on IL 394. About 14 miles ahead, turn left on West Goodenow Road and then turn left on Dutton Road. Follow signs to the campground.
UTM coordinates: 16T, 449447 E, 4583330 N
About the campground: Upon arriving at Goodenow Grove, you may want to survey the surrounding terrain by taking a trip up the sledding hill near the nature center. This will give you a taste of the forest preserve's rolling hills, open grasslands, and wooded ravines. The campgrounds offer both open and wooded camping spots. All camping areas are flat, and some are wonderfully private. The hiking trail alongside Plum Creek should not be overlooked.

44 Willow Slough Fish and Wildlife Area

Location: On the Illinois-Indiana border about 60 miles southeast of Joliet
Season: Year-round
Sites: 75 sites with no hookups
Maximum length: 40 feet
Facilities: Flush toilets, grills, showers, water, tables, dump station, picnic shelter
Fee per night: $$
Management: Indiana Department of Natural Resources
Contact: (219) 285-2704; www.in.gov/dnr/fishwild/3080.htm
Finding the campground: From I-57 in Kankakee, head east on IL 17. Turn right on IL 1. In St. Anne, where IL 1 takes a sharp right, turn left on West Guertin Street (CR 23). Keep straight

ahead for about 10 miles as this road changes its name several times. Turn right where the road ends. This road is the Indiana-Illinois state line and goes by both CR 700 West and CR 18000 East. The main entrance is on the left. Follow signs to the park office. The campground is just beyond the office.

UTM coordinates: 16T, 456553 E, 4535546 N

About the campground: There's much to explore among Willow Slough's 10,000 acres of sandy hills, oak savannas, ponds, and wetlands. The wooded campground hugs the shore of a 1,200-acre lake, and a large pond is just a short walk away. Anglers and hunters come to Willow Slough in equal measure. An extensive network of two-track roads throughout the park offers plenty of options for hikers.

One of the many pine plantations at Marengo Ridge Conservation Area.

The Great Prairie

Outdoor recreation in this part of the state often involves rods, reels, and hooks. Many anglers launch their boats in Lake Shelbyville—more than 11,000 acres in size and surrounded by hundreds of campsites. The quiet inlets along the lake's wooded shore offer top-notch fishing. Clinton Lake is another big watery attraction in this part of the state where anglers pursue catfish, bass, crappie, and other types of game fish.

The wide-open prairies within this part of Illinois produced the state's most famous resident, the sixteenth U.S. president. Tourism bureaus throughout the area are grateful that Lincoln visited so many local courthouses as a lawyer. And, of course, the state capital of Springfield contains museums and a roster of historic landmarks relating Lincoln's career as a state politician. The early life of Illinois' most famous son receives full treatment at Lincoln's New Salem State Historic Site, which contains a rebuilt version of the rural village where Lincoln spent his young adult years and first ran for state office.

Another local destination worth a visit is the town of Arthur, the heart of Illinois Amish country. Within Arthur and throughout the nearby countryside, visitors will find Amish bakeries and buggy repair shops, restaurants serving hearty Amish cooking, and stores that sell Amish furniture and handicrafts. Throughout the planting season, you're likely to see Amish men and women working the fields using horse-drawn farm implements.

While it's true that this part of Illinois is most known for its corn and soy plants and a topography that varies between flat and flatter, it's also true that there are plenty of lovely parks, lakes, and recreation areas within striking distance of the mid-state cities of Bloomington, Champaign, Danville, Decatur, and Springfield. Along with a generous number of state parks, this part of the state offers more than its share of smaller campgrounds within municipal parks. While some of these smaller parks offer minimal facilities, others posses an array of recreational opportunities.

The Bloomington-Champaign Area

		Hookup Sites	Total Sites	Max RV Length	Hookups	Toilets	Showers	Drinking Water	Dump Station	Recreation	Fee	Reservations
45	Livingston County Fairgrounds	25	25	40	E, W	F	Y	Y	Y		$$	N
46	Comlara County Park	94	128	40	E	F	Y	Y	Y	B, F, H, L, C	$$–$$$	Y
47	Moraine View State Recreation Area	137	170	40	E	F	Y	Y	Y	B, F, H, L, R	$–$$$	Y
48	Gibson City South Park	8	8	45	E, W	F	Y	Y	Y		$$	N
49	Clinton Lake State Recreation Area	303	308	45	E, W	F	Y	Y	Y	B, F, H, L	$$–$$$	Y
50	Weldon Springs State Park	75	90	40	E	F	Y	Y	Y	B, H, L	$–$$	Y
51	Friends Creek Regional Park	36	36	40	E	F	Y	Y	Y	B, F, H, L	$$	Y
52	Lodge Park County Forest Preserve	0	20	50	N/A	NF	N	Y	N	H, F	$	N

45 Livingston County Fairgrounds

Location: 50 miles southwest of Kankakee
Season: Apr to Nov
Sites: 25 sites with water and electrical hookups
Maximum length: 40 feet
Facilities: Flush toilets, grills, showers, water, tables, dump station, fairgrounds
Fee per night: $$
Management: Livingston County Agricultural Fair Association
Contact: (815) 844-5131; Pontiac Chamber of Commerce
Finding the campground: From I-55 north of Pontiac, exit south on IL 23. Turn right on 4-H Park Road. The campground is on the right.
UTM coordinates: 16T, 359657 E, 4528029 N
About the campground: Situated at the Livingston County Fairgrounds, this tiny campground is geared toward function. The campground sits next to the fair's livestock barns on a grassy lawn sprinkled with stately oaks. (The fair is typically held in mid-July.) In the nearby town of Pontiac, visit the Route 66 museum, several historic homes on display, or one of the parks with attractive swinging bridges crossing the Vermillion River.

The Great Prairie

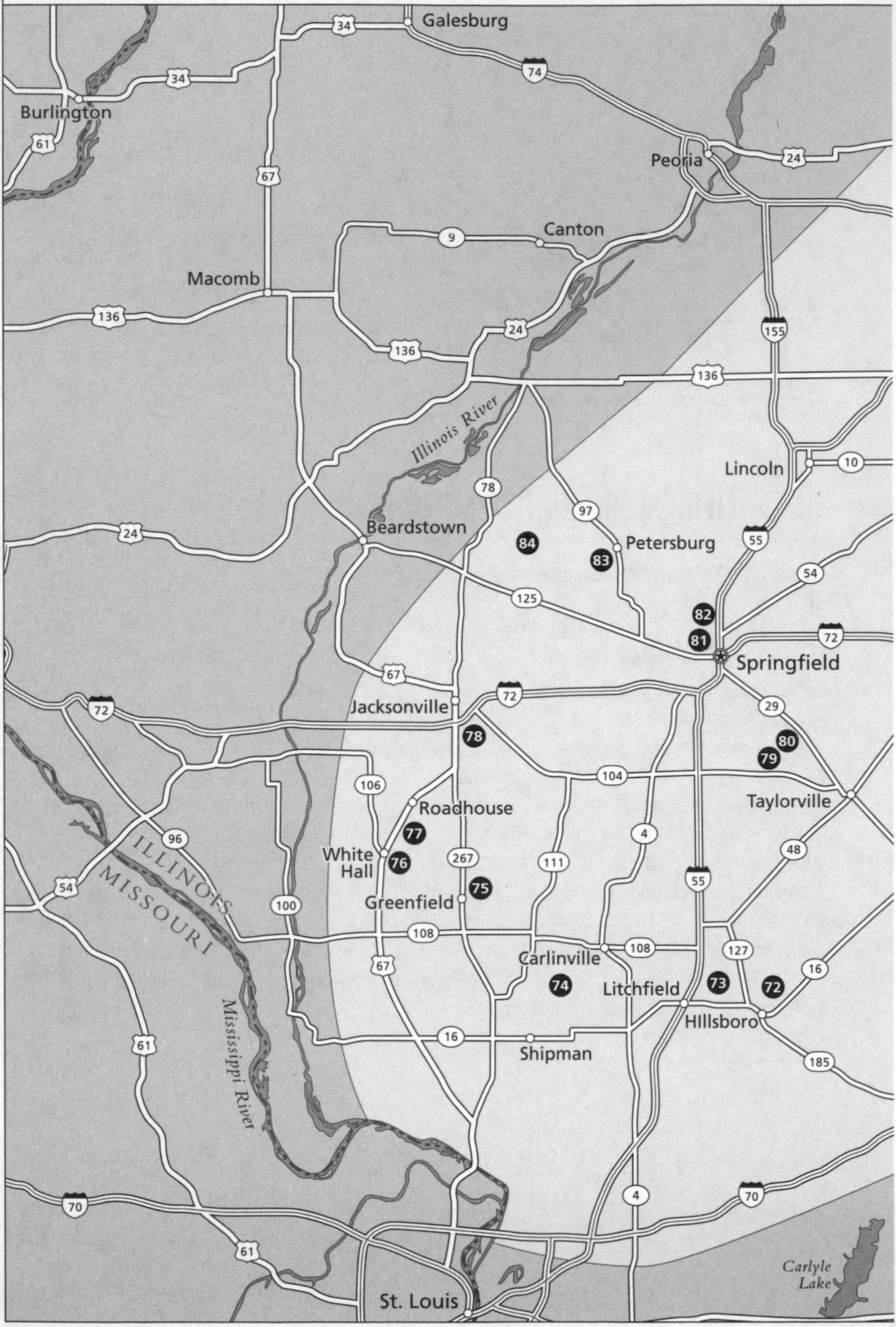

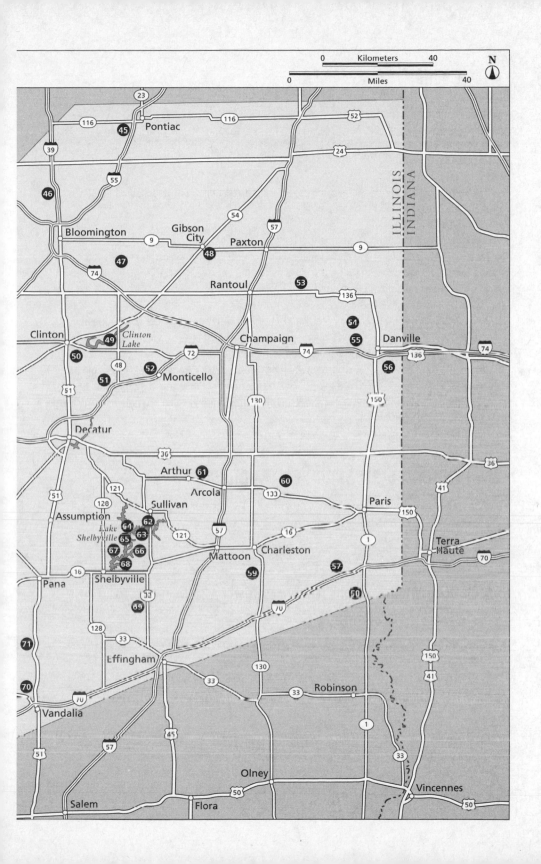

46 Comlara County Park

Location: About 8 miles north of Bloomington
Season: Year-round
Sites: 94 sites with electrical hookups (1 wheelchair-accessible), 23 sites with no hookups, 11 walk-in sites
Maximum length: 40 feet
Facilities: Flush toilets, water, showers, tables, grills, dump station, trails, beach, boat launch, picnicking facilities, boat rental, beach, playground
Fee per night: $$-$$$
Management: McLean County Department of Parks and Recreation
Contact: (309) 726-2022 (ext. 21); www.mcleancountyil.gov/parks; reservations accepted
Finding the campground: From I-39 north of Bloomington, exit on CR 8 (CR 2500 North) and head west. Turn left on Comlara Park Road and enter the park.
UTM coordinates: 16T, 328158 E, 328158 N
About the campground: Take in views of the many-armed Evergreen Lake from the campground's open, rolling terrain. Hickory and oak trees provide shade for most of the campsites. Large walk-in sites are located right on the water. Visitors often come for the park's prime fishing waters and easy access to Bloomington. They also come for more than 20 miles of hiking and mountain biking trails that wind through the park's 2,200 acres of wooded terrain surrounding the lake. Since the county owns the lake (it serves as a water supply) and all the adjoining property, you won't see any private residences on the lake.

47 Moraine View State Recreation Area

Location: About 15 miles southeast of Bloomington
Season: Year-round
Sites: 137 sites with electrical hookups, 33 walk-in sites
Maximum length: 40 feet
Facilities: Flush toilets, water, tables, grills, showers, dump station, picnic areas, boat launch, restaurant, hiking trails, horse rental and camping, fishing piers, boat rental, playground
Fee per night: $-$$$
Management: Illinois Department of Natural Resources
Contact: (309) 724-8032; http://dnr.state.il.us/lands/landmgt/parks/r3/moraine.htm; reservations accepted
Finding the campground: From I-74, take exit 149 and follow CR 21 (South Chestnut Street) north into LeRoy. In LeRoy, turn left on US 150, and then turn right on LeRoy-Lexington Blacktop (CR 21). Turn right at the sign for the park.
UTM coordinates: 16T, 354054 E, 4475261 N
About the campground: As you follow the curvy, rolling park road that loops around the 158-acre lake at Moraine View Recreation Area, you'll pass through prairie and thick groves of cottonwood, maple, and sumac. You'll also catch glimpses of the enormous wind turbines that are part of the

52 Lodge Park County Forest Preserve

Location: About 20 miles southwest of Champaign
Season: Beginning of Apr 1 to beginning of Dec 1 (open year-round to hike-in campers)
Sites: 20 sites with no hookups
Maximum length: 50 feet
Facilities: Vault toilets, water, tables, grills, playground, small fishing pond
Fee per night: $
Management: Piatt County Forest Preserve District
Contact: (217) 762-4531
Finding the campground: On I-72 just north of Monticello, take IL 105 north. The park is immediately on the left.
UTM coordinates: 16T, 366588 E, 4435725 N
About the campground: The camping area at Lodge Park occupies a big grassy lawn that is well shaded with large oak trees. West of the camping area and down the ravine, the Sangamon River wriggles and loops through dense bottomland woods. While the park offers minimal amenities, plenty of attractions beckon from the surrounding area: the Monticello Railway Museum; a historic district in Monticello; and Allerton Park, a 1,500-acre former estate with hiking trails, formal gardens, and more than one hundred sculptures.

Twin Groves Wind Farm. The park's main camping area is open, gently rolling, and mostly shaded. Two walk-in camping areas on the other side of the lake require varying walk-in distances: Catfish Bay sites are in a wooded area close to the parking area and the lake; the Tall Timber sites require longer hikes, but offer more seclusion within dense bottomland woods. A horse stable rents horses to ride on 10 miles of bridle paths within the park.

48 Gibson City South Park

Location: About 25 miles north of Champaign
Season: Open from the beginning of Apr to the end of Oct
Sites: 8 sites with water and electrical hookups
Maximum length: 45 feet
Facilities: Flush toilets, water, tables, grills, dump station, paved RV pads, playground, picnic shelter, showers (shower key must be picked up from police station)
Fee per night: $$ (pay at police station or chamber of commerce)
Management: City of Gibson
Contact: (217) 784-5872
Finding the campground: South Park is located on IL 9 in Gibson City, 2 blocks east of its junction with IL 47.
UTM coordinates: 16T, 383560 E, 4479194 N
About the campground: This tiny municipal park, located in a small town, is within a stone's throw of several restaurants and 6 blocks from a pleasant downtown square. The shaded campsites sit on a grassy lawn behind a display of a railroad steam engine from 1850. Just outside of Gibson City, the Harvest Moon Drive-In is a local landmark that hosts first-run films.

49 Clinton Lake State Recreation Area

Location: About 20 miles south of Bloomington
Season: Year-round
Sites: 17 sites with water and electrical hookups, 200 sites with electrical hookups, 5 sites with no hookups
Maximum length: 45 feet
Facilities: Flush toilets, water, tables, grills, dump station, showers, boat launch, boat rental, beach, concessions, hiking trails, picnic areas, playground
Fee per night: $$-$$$
Management: Illinois Department of Natural Resources
Contact: (217) 935-8722; reservations accepted; http://dnr.state.il.us/lands/landmgt/parks/r3/clinton.htm
Finding the campground: On I-74 between Bloomington and Champaign, take IL 54 southwest nearly 10 miles to CR 20 (CR 920 North). Turn left and pass through DeWitt. Follow signs into the park on the right.

Clinton Lake is fringed with a wooded shoreline.

UTM coordinates: 16T, 347730 E, 4447022 N
About the campground: The sprawling campground at Clinton Lake has numerous cul-de-sacs, giving it the feel of a suburban neighborhood. Some sections of the campground are wooded; other parts offer little shade and sit within an attractive savanna with prairie grasses and swaths of wetland. The many boats parked at the campsites reveal Clinton Lake's primary draw. The 4,900-acre, human-made lake stretches about 16 miles and through some 9,000 acres of mostly wooded state parkland. Water skiers and power boaters hang out in the south end of the lake while people canoeing or sailing stick toward the north end.

50 Weldon Springs State Park

Location: About 15 miles north of Decatur
Season: Year-round
Sites: 75 sites with electrical hookups, 9 walk-in sites, 6 backpacking sites
Maximum length: 40 feet

Facilities: Flush toilets, water, tables, grills, dump station, showers, hiking trails, playground, boat launch, boat rental, sports fields and courts, concessions, restaurant, playground
Fee per night: $–$$
Management: Illinois Department of Natural Resources
Contact: (217) 935-2644; http://dnr.state.il.us/lands/Landmgt/parks/r3/weldonra.htm; reservations accepted
Finding the campground: From I-55 south of Bloomington, head south on US 51. In Clinton, turn left on IL 10. Follow signs to the park. From I-72 north of Decatur, head north on US 51. Before Clinton, turn right on CR 250 North and follow signs.
UTM coordinates: 16T, 335908 E, 4442856 N
About the campground: In the early twentieth century, Weldon Springs served as the site for popular annual chautauquas, which brought people from the region to see speakers and entertainers. Now the park hosts a bevy of recreational activities—many geared toward families. The campground, a short walk from the park's small lake, sits within a well-shaded, lightly rolling area fringed by stands of large oak and hickory trees. Explore the old schoolhouse/museum within the park, as well as a half-dozen trails, some of which have interpretive brochures and signs. The best trails are the Lakeside Interpretive Trail, which loops around the lake, and the Schoolhouse Trail, which runs through prairie and passes eighty bluebird houses.

51 Friends Creek Regional Park

Location: About 15 miles northeast of Decatur
Season: Beginning of Apr 1 to the end of Oct 31
Sites: 36 sites with electrical hookups
Maximum length: 40 feet
Facilities: Flush toilets, water, tables, grills, dump station, showers, hiking trails, picnic areas, playground
Fee per night: $$
Management: Macon County Conservation District
Contact: (217) 423-7708; www.maconcountyconservation.org; reservations accepted
Finding the campground: About 10 miles west of Monticello, exit I-72 and head north on IL 48. Turn left on Duroc Road, and then turn right on Friends Creek Park Road. From I-74 to the north, take IL 54 southwest to IL 48. Turn left on IL 48. Turn right on East Washington Road, and then turn left on Friends Creek Road.
UTM coordinates: 16T, 348017 E, 4432487 N
About the campground: Friends Creek Regional Park is a gem of a place hardly known outside of the immediate area. Most likely, you'll share this campground mainly with the local wildlife. The open, grassy camping area is shaded by a constellation of towering oaks. The 526-acre park contains prairie, savanna, and bottomland woods along two winding arms of Friends Creek. The Woodland Trail offers a shady, 2-mile ramble along Friends Creek and passes by a restored one-room schoolhouse from the 1890s.

The Danville Area

		Hookup Sites	Total Sites	Max RV Length	Hookups	Toilets	Showers	Drinking Water	Dump Station	Recreation	Fee	Reservations
53	Middle Fork River Forest Preserve	53	65	40	E	F	Y	Y	Y	F, H	$$	Y
54	Middle Fork State Fish and Wildlife Area	0	21	45	N/A	NF	N	Y	Y	F, H, R, L	$	N
55	Kickapoo State Park	90	187	40	E	F	Y	Y	Y	B, F, H, L, R	$-$$$	N
56	Forest Glen County Preserve	34	56	40	E	F	Y	Y	Y	B, H, L	$$-$$$	Y

53 Middle Fork River Forest Preserve

Location: About 25 miles northeast of Champaign
Season: Year-round
Sites: 53 sites with electrical hookups, 12 sites with no hookups
Maximum length: 40 feet
Facilities: Flush toilets, water, tables, grills, showers, dump station, fishing piers, beach, picnic shelters, playground, volleyball court, hiking trails
Fee per night: $$
Management: Champaign County Forest Preserve District
Contact: (217) 586-3360; http://www.ccfpd.org/attractions/harry_swartz_campground.html; reservations accepted
Finding the campground: If coming from the south, exit I-57 on US 136 and head east through Rantoul. In Penfield, go north on CR 2700 East. The park is on the left. From the north, exit I-57 on IL 9 and go east through Paxton. Turn right on CR 2700 East. The park is on the right.
UTM coordinates: 16T, 419271 E, 4469690 N
About the campground: Among Middle Fork River Forest Preserve's prized possessions are the restored prairie and savanna, where flowers like goldenrod, thistle, and compass plants thrive. The park also contains large patches of marshland and many wooded areas heavy with oak, hickory, walnut, and hackberry trees. The campsites—located in both woodland and savanna—are ample, and most have a buffer of greenery between them. Don't miss the trails that run for several miles through bottomland woods and alongside the middle fork branch of the Vermillion River and Sugar Creek.

54 Middle Fork State Fish and Wildlife Area

Location: About 7 miles west of Danville
Season: Year-round
Sites: 15 sites with no hookups, 6 backpacking sites

Maximum length: 45 feet
Facilities: Vault toilets, water, tables, grills, dump station, hiking/snowmobiling/equestrian trails, picnicking areas, canoe launch
Fee per night: $
Management: Illinois Department of Natural Resources
Contact: (217) 442-4915; http://dnr.state.il.us/lands/Landmgt/parks/r3/middle.htm
Finding the campground: From I-74 west of Danville, take CR 10 north (exit 206). Keep straight ahead on 900 East Road as CR 10 veers left. Turn right on CR 2250 North and follow the signs.
UTM coordinates: 16T, 436963 E, 4449805 N
About the campground: Middle Fork Fish and Wildlife Area caters mostly to equestrian campers, but there are a number sites available for general use. The open, grassy camping areas sit in the shade of large oak trees. A quarter mile down the road from the campground is a canoe launch on the Middle Fork branch of the Vermillion River. When water levels are high enough in spring and early summer, this stretch of the Middle Fork offers one of Illinois' most scenic paddling experiences. Rent your gear and arrange a shuttle in Kickapoo State Park.

55 Kickapoo State Park

Location: About 5 miles west of Danville
Season: Year-round
Sites: 90 sites with electrical hookups, 80 sites with no hookups, 17 walk-in sites
Maximum length: 40 feet
Facilities: Flush toilets, water, tables, grills, dump station, showers, hiking and mountain biking trails, boat and canoe rental, boat launches, restaurant, fishing piers, numerous lakes and ponds, picnicking areas, riding stable
Fee per night: $-$$$
Management: Illinois Department of Natural Resources
Contact: (217) 442-4915; http://dnr.state.il.us/lands/landmgt/parks/r3/kickapoo.htm
Finding the campground: From I-74 west of Danville, take CR 10 north (exit 206). Turn right on Glenburn Creek Road and follow signs to the park. The entrance to the campground is on the right.
UTM coordinates: 16T, 436846 E, 4442889 N
About the campground: It's hard to believe that all the scenic lakes and wooded hills at Kickapoo State Park were once home to an extensive strip-mining operation. Now that the prairie, ponds, and hilly woodland have been restored, it's one of the most popular state parks in central Illinois. The area of the campground catering to RVs is wooded and shady; the tent camping area occupies a mostly shaded grassy expanse above one of the many ponds at the park. Some visitors will be disappointed to discover that the campground is within earshot of both I-74 and the nearby fairgrounds, where motorized races are regularly held. Making up for that are the dramatic wooded bluffs, dozens of ponds and lakes, and one of the most scenic rivers in the state.

Twin Groves Wind Farm. The park's main camping area is open, gently rolling, and mostly shaded. Two walk-in camping areas on the other side of the lake require varying walk-in distances: Catfish Bay sites are in a wooded area close to the parking area and the lake; the Tall Timber sites require longer hikes, but offer more seclusion within dense bottomland woods. A horse stable rents horses to ride on 10 miles of bridle paths within the park.

48 Gibson City South Park

Location: About 25 miles north of Champaign
Season: Open from the beginning of Apr to the end of Oct
Sites: 8 sites with water and electrical hookups
Maximum length: 45 feet
Facilities: Flush toilets, water, tables, grills, dump station, paved RV pads, playground, picnic shelter, showers (shower key must be picked up from police station)
Fee per night: $$ (pay at police station or chamber of commerce)
Management: City of Gibson
Contact: (217) 784-5872
Finding the campground: South Park is located on IL 9 in Gibson City, 2 blocks east of its junction with IL 47.
UTM coordinates: 10T, 383560 E, 4479194 N
About the campground: This tiny municipal park, located in a small town, is within a stone's throw of several restaurants and 6 blocks from a pleasant downtown square. The shaded campsites sit on a grassy lawn behind a display of a railroad steam engine from 1850. Just outside of Gibson City, the Harvest Moon Drive-In is a local landmark that hosts first-run films.

49 Clinton Lake State Recreation Area

Location: About 20 miles south of Bloomington
Season: Year-round
Sites: 17 sites with water and electrical hookups, 286 sites with electrical hookups, 5 sites with no hookups
Maximum length: 45 feet
Facilities: Flush toilets, water, tables, grills, dump station, showers, boat launch, boat rental, beach, concessions, hiking trails, picnic areas, playground
Fee per night: $$-$$$
Management: Illinois Department of Natural Resources
Contact: (217) 935-8722; reservations accepted; http://dnr.state.il.us/lands/landmgt/parks/r3/clinton.htm
Finding the campground: On I-74 between Bloomington and Champaign, take IL 54 southwest nearly 10 miles to CR 20 (CR 920 North). Turn left and pass through DeWitt. Follow signs into the park on the right.

Clinton Lake is fringed with a wooded shoreline.

UTM coordinates: 16T, 347730 E, 4447022 N

About the campground: The sprawling campground at Clinton Lake has numerous cul-de-sacs, giving it the feel of a suburban neighborhood. Some sections of the campground are wooded; other parts offer little shade and sit within an attractive savanna with prairie grasses and swaths of wetland. The many boats parked at the campsites reveal Clinton Lake's primary draw. The 4,900-acre, human-made lake stretches about 16 miles and through some 9,000 acres of mostly wooded state parkland. Water skiers and power boaters hang out in the south end of the lake while people canoeing or sailing stick toward the north end.

50 Weldon Springs State Park

Location: About 15 miles north of Decatur
Season: Year-round
Sites: 75 sites with electrical hookups, 9 walk-in sites, 6 backpacking sites
Maximum length: 40 feet

Facilities: Flush toilets, water, tables, grills, dump station, showers, hiking trails, playground, boat launch, boat rental, sports fields and courts, concessions, restaurant, playground
Fee per night: $–$$
Management: Illinois Department of Natural Resources
Contact: (217) 935-2644; http://dnr.state.il.us/lands/Landmgt/parks/r3/weldonra.htm; reservations accepted
Finding the campground: From I-55 south of Bloomington, head south on US 51. In Clinton, turn left on IL 10. Follow signs to the park. From I-72 north of Decatur, head north on US 51. Before Clinton, turn right on CR 250 North and follow signs.
UTM coordinates: 16T, 335908 E, 4442856 N
About the campground: In the early twentieth century, Weldon Springs served as the site for popular annual chautauquas, which brought people from the region to see speakers and entertainers. Now the park hosts a bevy of recreational activities—many geared toward families. The campground, a short walk from the park's small lake, sits within a well-shaded, lightly rolling area fringed by stands of large oak and hickory trees. Explore the old schoolhouse/museum within the park, as well as a half-dozen trails, some of which have interpretive brochures and signs. The best trails are the Lakeside Interpretive Trail, which loops around the lake, and the Schoolhouse Trail, which runs through prairie and passes eighty bluebird houses.

51 Friends Creek Regional Park

Location: About 15 miles northeast of Decatur
Season: Beginning of Apr 1 to the end of Oct 31
Sites: 36 sites with electrical hookups
Maximum length: 40 feet
Facilities: Flush toilets, water, tables, grills, dump station, showers, hiking trails, picnic areas, playground
Fee per night: $$
Management: Macon County Conservation District
Contact: (217) 423-7708; www.maconcountyconservation.org; reservations accepted
Finding the campground: About 10 miles west of Monticello, exit I-72 and head north on IL 48. Turn left on Duroc Road, and then turn right on Friends Creek Park Road. From I-74 to the north, take IL 54 southwest to IL 48. Turn left on IL 48. Turn right on East Washington Road, and then turn left on Friends Creek Road.
UTM ooordinates: 16T, 348017 E, 4432487 N
About the campground: Friends Creek Regional Park is a gem of a place hardly known outside of the immediate area. Most likely, you'll share this campground mainly with the local wildlife. The open, grassy camping area is shaded by a constellation of towering oaks. The 526-acre park contains prairie, savanna, and bottomland woods along two winding arms of Friends Creek. The Woodland Trail offers a shady, 2-mile ramble along Friends Creek and passes by a restored one-room schoolhouse from the 1890s.

52 Lodge Park County Forest Preserve

Location: About 20 miles southwest of Champaign
Season: Beginning of Apr 1 to beginning of Dec 1 (open year-round to hike-in campers)
Sites: 20 sites with no hookups
Maximum length: 50 feet
Facilities: Vault toilets, water, tables, grills, playground, small fishing pond
Fee per night: $
Management: Piatt County Forest Preserve District
Contact: (217) 762-4531
Finding the campground: On I-72 just north of Monticello, take IL 105 north. The park is immediately on the left.
UTM coordinates: 16T, 366588 E, 4435725 N
About the campground: The camping area at Lodge Park occupies a big grassy lawn that is well shaded with large oak trees. West of the camping area and down the ravine, the Sangamon River wriggles and loops through dense bottomland woods. While the park offers minimal amenities, plenty of attractions beckon from the surrounding area: the Monticello Railway Museum; a historic district in Monticello; and Allerton Park, a 1,500-acre former estate with hiking trails, formal gardens, and more than one hundred sculptures.

The Danville Area

		Hookup Sites	Total Sites	Max RV Length	Hookups	Toilets	Showers	Drinking Water	Dump Station	Recreation	Fee	Reservations
53	Middle Fork River Forest Preserve	53	65	40	E	F	Y	Y	Y	F, H	$$	Y
54	Middle Fork State Fish and Wildlife Area	0	21	45	N/A	NF	N	Y	Y	F, H, R, L	$	N
55	Kickapoo State Park	90	187	40	E	F	Y	Y	Y	B, F, H, L, R	$-$$$	N
56	Forest Glen County Preserve	34	56	40	E	F	Y	Y	Y	B, H, L	$$-$$$	Y

53 Middle Fork River Forest Preserve

Location: About 25 miles northeast of Champaign
Season: Year-round
Sites: 53 sites with electrical hookups, 12 sites with no hookups
Maximum length: 40 feet
Facilities: Flush toilets, water, tables, grills, showers, dump station, fishing piers, beach, picnic shelters, playground, volleyball court, hiking trails
Fee per night: $$
Management: Champaign County Forest Preserve District
Contact: (217) 586-3360; http://www.ccfpd.org/attractions/harry_swartz_campground.html; reservations accepted
Finding the campground: If coming from the south, exit I-57 on US 136 and head east through Rantoul. In Penfield, go north on CR 2700 East. The park is on the left. From the north, exit I-57 on IL 9 and go east through Paxton. Turn right on CR 2700 East. The park is on the right.
UTM coordinates: 16T, 419271 E, 4469690 N
About the campground: Among Middle Fork River Forest Preserve's prized possessions are the restored prairie and savanna, where flowers like goldenrod, thistle, and compass plants thrive. The park also contains large patches of marshland and many wooded areas heavy with oak, hickory, walnut, and hackberry trees. The campsites—located in both woodland and savanna—are ample, and most have a buffer of greenery between them. Don't miss the trails that run for several miles through bottomland woods and alongside the middle fork branch of the Vermillion River and Sugar Creek.

54 Middle Fork State Fish and Wildlife Area

Location: About 7 miles west of Danville
Season: Year-round
Sites: 15 sites with no hookups, 6 backpacking sites

Maximum length: 45 feet
Facilities: Vault toilets, water, tables, grills, dump station, hiking/snowmobiling/equestrian trails, picnicking areas, canoe launch
Fee per night: $
Management: Illinois Department of Natural Resources
Contact: (217) 442-4915; http://dnr.state.il.us/lands/Landmgt/parks/r3/middle.htm
Finding the campground: From I-74 west of Danville, take CR 10 north (exit 206). Keep straight ahead on 900 East Road as CR 10 veers left. Turn right on CR 2250 North and follow the signs.
UTM coordinates: 16T, 436963 E, 4449805 N
About the campground: Middle Fork Fish and Wildlife Area caters mostly to equestrian campers, but there are a number sites available for general use. The open, grassy camping areas sit in the shade of large oak trees. A quarter mile down the road from the campground is a canoe launch on the Middle Fork branch of the Vermillion River. When water levels are high enough in spring and early summer, this stretch of the Middle Fork offers one of Illinois' most scenic paddling experiences. Rent your gear and arrange a shuttle in Kickapoo State Park.

55 Kickapoo State Park

Location: About 5 miles west of Danville
Season: Year-round
Sites: 90 sites with electrical hookups, 80 sites with no hookups, 17 walk-in sites
Maximum length: 40 feet
Facilities: Flush toilets, water, tables, grills, dump station, showers, hiking and mountain biking trails, boat and canoe rental, boat launches, restaurant, fishing piers, numerous lakes and ponds, picnicking areas, riding stable
Fee per night: $-$$$
Management: Illinois Department of Natural Resources
Contact: (217) 442-4915; http://dnr.state.il.us/lands/landmgt/parks/r3/kickapoo.htm
Finding the campground: From I-74 west of Danville, take CR 10 north (exit 206). Turn right on Glenburn Creek Road and follow signs to the park. The entrance to the campground is on the right.
UTM coordinates: 16T, 436846 E, 4442889 N
About the campground: It's hard to believe that all the scenic lakes and wooded hills at Kickapoo State Park were once home to an extensive strip-mining operation. Now that the prairie, ponds, and hilly woodland have been restored, it's one of the most popular state parks in central Illinois. The area of the campground catering to RVs is wooded and shady; the tent camping area occupies a mostly shaded grassy expanse above one of the many ponds at the park. Some visitors will be disappointed to discover that the campground is within earshot of both I-74 and the nearby fairgrounds, where motorized races are regularly held. Making up for that are the dramatic wooded bluffs, dozens of ponds and lakes, and one of the most scenic rivers in the state.

One of the many ponds at Kickapoo State Park that were reclaimed from strip mining.

56 Forest Glen County Preserve

Location: About 8 miles southeast of Danville
Season: Year-round
Sites: 34 sites with electrical hookups, 8 sites with no hookups, 14 walk-in sites, several backpacking sites
Maximum length: 40 feet
Facilities: Flush toilets, water, tables, grills, dump station, picnicking areas, hiking trails, showers, arboretum, canoe launch
Fee per night: $$–$$$
Management: Vermillion County Forest Preserve District
Contact: (217) 662-2142; http://www.vccd.org/recreation.html; reservations accepted
Finding the campground: From I-74 south of Danville, head south on US 150/IL 1. In Westville, take Main Street left. Follow CR 5 for 7 miles, following signs to the park.
UTM coordinates: 16T, 452120 E, 4428802 N
About the campground: The main campground occupies a shaded grassy area at the edge of a pleasant pond. For visitors who want to experience the deep woods without schlepping a backpack, the walk-in sites at Forest Glen are some of the best around. The well-spaced sites sit in a thick grove of maples and are perched on the edge of a ravine. Prairie, savanna, and pine plantations appear in other parts of the park, as do an old pioneer homestead exhibit and a nature center with live animal displays. This unusual county park also contains a facility for growing shitake mushrooms and an arboretum where visitors can walk among hundreds of native and nonnative trees, shrubs, ornamentals, and conifers.

From Lake Shelbyville to the East

		Hookup Sites	Total Sites	Max RV Length	Hookups	Toilets	Showers	Drinking Water	Dump Station	Recreation	Fee	Reservations
57	Mill Creek County Park	139	147	40	E	F	Y	Y	Y	B, H, F, L, R	$$	Y
58	Lincoln Trail State Park	180	200	40	E	F	Y	Y	Y	B, H, F	$-$$$	N
59	Fox Ridge State Park	43	43	40	E	F	Y	Y	Y	H, L	$$	Y
60	Walnut Point State Fish and Wildlife Area	34	54	40	E	F	Y	Y	Y	H, F, L	$-$$	Y
61	Arthur RV Park	5	5	30	E	F	N	Y	Y	S	$$	N
62	Forest "Bo" Woods Recreation Area	76	76	40	E, W	F	Y	Y	Y	F, L	$$	Y
63	Opossum Creek Recreation Area	58	80	45	E	F	Y	Y	Y	F, L	$$	Y
64	Eagle Creek State Park	148	103	40	E	F	Y	Y	Y	H, F, L	$-$$	Y
65	Wolf Creek State Park	304	382	40	E	F	Y	Y	Y	H, F, L, S	$-$$$	Y
66	Lone Point Recreation Area	91	98	40	E	F	Y	Y	Y	H, F, L	$$	Y
67	Coon Creek Recreation Area	202	202	45	E, W	F	Y	Y	Y	H, F, L, S	$$	Y
68	Lithia Springs Recreation Area	123	123	40	E, W	F	Y	Y	Y	F, L, S	$$	Y
69	Hidden Springs State Forest	0	25	40	N/A	F	N	Y	Y	H, F	$	N

57 Mill Creek County Park

Location: About 45 miles south of Danville
Season: Open from beginning of Apr to end of Oct
Sites: 139 sites with electrical hookups, 8 walk-in sites
Maximum length: 40 feet
Facilities: Flush toilets, water, tables, grills, dump station, showers, hiking/ATV/horse trails, horseshoe pits, volleyball and basketball courts, nature center, playground, boat launch, sports fields, picnic shelters, boat and cabin rentals
Fee per night: $$
Management: Clark County Park District
Contact: (217) 889-3601; www.clarkcountyparkdistrict.com/millcreek; reservations accepted
Finding the campground: From I-70 near Martinsville, head north at exit 136 on North Cleone Road (CR 700 East). About 7 miles ahead, turn right on East Clarksville Road. The park is on the right.
UTM coordinates: 16S, 430093 E, 4366184 N
About the campground: Visitors come to Mill Creek Lake for the good fishing and a lively campground. They also come to enjoy the lake's attractive vistas and its thickly wooded shores. Camping at Mill Creek takes place in a large, flat, open area; about half of the campsites are unshaded. Sites with some privacy and plenty of shade are situated on the far side, opposite the campground entrance road. Several miles of hiking trails may yield sightings of beaver cuttings, dozens of species of wildflowers, and, at certain times of the year, bald eagles and ospreys.

58 Lincoln Trail State Park

Location: About 50 miles northeast of Effingham
Season: Year-round
Sites: 180 sites with electrical hookups, 20 sites with no hookups
Maximum length: 40 feet
Facilities: Flush toilets, water, tables, grills, dump station, showers, hiking trails, restaurant, concessionaire, boat rentals, fishing piers
Fee per night: $–$$$
Management: Illinois Department of Natural Resources
Contact: (217) 826-2222; http://dnr.state.il.us/lands/landmgt/parks/r3/Lincoln.htm
Finding the campground: From I-70 north of Marshall, drive south on IL 1. Turn right on East 1350th Road and follow signs for the park.
UTM coordinates: 16S, 438313 E, 4354587 N
About the campground: Named after the local route that Abraham Lincoln's family followed from Indiana to Illinois in 1831, this 1,000-acre park contains an attractive, many-fingered lake. The large RV camping area is flat and fairly open with ample shade provided by plantings of oak and maple. The tent camping area occupies a maple forest on a bluff above the lake. Some of these sites border ravines, and some are situated on a little peninsula jutting into the lake. Next to the campgrounds is an Illinois nature preserve containing deep ravines overflowing with a beech-maple forest that has changed little from the days when Lincoln and his family traveled through the area.

59 Fox Ridge State Park

Location: About 8 miles south of Charleston
Season: Year-round
Sites: 43 sites with electrical hookups, 3 rustic cabins
Maximum length: 40 feet
Facilities: Flush toilets, water, tables, grills, dump station, showers, picnicking shelters, hiking trails, canoe launches, playground
Fee per night: $$
Management: Illinois Department of Natural Resources
Contact: (217) 345-6416; http://dnr.state.il.us/lands/landmgt/parks/r3/fox/fox.htm; reservations accepted
Finding the campground: From I-57 near Mattoon, head east on IL 16. In Charleston, turn right on IL 130. The park is on the right.
UTM coordinates: 16S, 401630 E, 4361735 N
About the campground: Set amidst rolling hills along the forested bluffs of the Embarras River, Fox Ridge State Park stands in sharp contrast to the flat prairies of most of this part of Illinois. The campground features well-spaced, fairly private sites shaded with maple and pine trees. The park's

extensive trail system takes hikers through wetland, savanna, ravines, and the bottomland woods along the shore of the Embarras (pronounced AM-braw). Two canoe launches within the park allow for local paddling trips. Visitors often make a stop nearby at the Lincoln Log Cabin State Historic Site, the farm where Abraham Lincoln's father and stepmother lived.

60 Walnut Point State Fish and Wildlife Area

Location: About 15 miles northeast of Charleston
Season: Year-round
Sites: 34 sites with electrical hookups, 20 walk-in camping sites
Maximum length: 40 feet
Facilities: Flush toilets, water, tables, grills, dump station, concessions, showers, boat launch, picnicking shelters, playgrounds, fishing piers, horseshoe pits, summer weekend concerts
Fee per night: $–$$
Management: Illinois Department of Natural Resources
Contact: (217) 346-3336; http://dnr.state.il.us/lands/landmgt/parks/r3/walnutpt.htm; reservations accepted
Finding the campground: As I-57 passes Arcola, exit east on IL 133. In Oakland, turn left on Walnut Street. The entrance to the park is several miles ahead on the left.
UTM coordinates: 16S, 411228 E, 4394886 N
About the campground: What this park lacks in size, it makes up with plenty of charm. The park is centered on the attractive multifingered lake; the south end of the park is bordered by the Embarras River. Prime picnicking spots are available on the shore of the lake. The roomy campsites in the main camping area are well shaded by stands of elm, maple, hickory, and a smattering of ash and pine trees. The well-distributed tent camping sites are located on a small peninsula right at the water's edge.

61 Arthur RV Park

Location: About 25 miles southeast of Decatur
Season: Year-round
Sites: 5 sites with electrical hookups
Maximum length: 30 feet
Facilities: Flush toilets, water, dump station, picnicking areas
Fee per night: $$
Management: Village of Arthur
Contact: (217) 543-2927
Finding the campground: As I-57 passes Arcola, head west on IL 133. In Arthur, turn left on South Spruce Street. The campground is located on the right between the back of the high school and the fairgrounds.
UTM coordinates: 16S, 374093 E, 4396197 N

About the campground: This tiny municipal RV campground sits behind the Arthur high school. The sites—mostly unshaded—are positioned alongside a community pool. This campground is located blocks from downtown Arthur, the center of Illinois Amish country. Dozens of businesses in Arthur and the surrounding countryside sell all sorts of Amish-made items, from baked goods to buggies.

62 Forest "Bo" Woods Recreation Area

Location: About 30 miles southeast of Decatur
Season: End of May to end of Oct
Sites: 62 sites with electrical hookups, 14 sites with water and electrical hookups
Maximum length: 40 feet
Facilities: Flush toilets, water, tables, grills, dump station, boat launch, fishing dock, fish cleaning station, laundry, playground, showers, pay telephone
Fee per night: $$
Management: U.S. Army Corps of Engineers
Contact: (217) 774-3951; www.mvs.usace.army.mil/Shelbyville/recreate.htm; (877) 444-6777 or www.recreation.gov for reservations
Finding the campground: From Decatur, head southeast on IL 121. In Sullivan, go south on IL 32. The entrance is on the right.
UTM coordinates: 16S, 360934 E, 4379308 N
About the campground: This recently remodeled campground is oriented heavily toward RV camping. Stately maple trees provide ample shade. Take in expansive views of Lake Shelbyville and nearby wetlands from the picnicking area set on a nearby peninsula. A few miles north, you'll find Amish goods in the town of Sullivan (the town serves as the southern edge of Illinois Amish country). South of the campground is Sullivan Beach.

63 Opossum Creek Recreation Area

Location: About 25 miles southeast of Decatur
Season: Beginning of May to beginning of Sept
Sites: 58 sites with electrical hookups, 22 sites with no hookups
Maximum length: 45 feet
Facilities: Flush toilets, water, tables, grills, dump station, showers, boat ramp, dock, fish-cleaning station, playground, telephone
Fee per night: $$
Management: U.S. Army Corps of Engineers
Contact: (217) 774-3951; www.mvs.usace.army.mil/Shelbyville/recreate.htm; www.recreation .gov or (877) 444-6777 for reservations
Finding the campground: From I-57 near Mattoon, head west on IL 16. In Shelbyville, go north on IL 128. Turn right on CR 1650 North; turn right again on CR 1800 East. Turn left on CR 1600 North.

UTM coordinates: 16S, 347428 E, 4367548 N

About the campground: Opossum Creek is one of the smaller camping areas on Lake Shelbyville; it's also one of the closest camping spots to the town of Shelbyville. The oak- and hickory-canopied campsites occupy a series of small peninsulas jutting into the lake. Many campsites are perched on modest-sized bluffs that offer fine views of the enormous lake and the nearby rolling terrain. Shelbyville hosts several attractive parks, a historic courthouse and library, and an old-time downtown movie theater.

64 Eagle Creek State Park

Location: About 30 miles southeast of Decatur
Season: All year except Dec
Sites: 148 sites with electrical hookups, 5 sites with no hookups, 10 walk-in sites
Maximum length: 40 feet
Facilities: Flush toilets, water, tables, grills, dump station, showers, hiking trails, picnicking areas, boat launch, resort and golf course
Fee per night: $–$$
Management: Illinois Department of Natural Resources
Contact: (217) 756-8260; http://dnr.state.il.us/lands/Landmgt/parks/r3/eaglecrk.htm; reservations accepted
Finding the campground: Head south from Decatur on US 51. Go left on CR 1200 North in Assumption. After passing through Findlay, turn right on 2200 East County Shelby Road and then turn left on CR 2030 North.
UTM coordinates: 16S, 353211 E, 4373357 N
About the campground: Eagle Creek State Park occupies a peninsula nearly 2 miles long in the midsection of Lake Shelbyville. The main camping area—open and partially shaded—is surrounded by an attractive savanna and prairie on one side and oak-hickory woods on the other. Eagle Creek contains the best tent-camping options among the seven campgrounds on Lake Shelbyville: The tent camping and walk-in sites, located 0.5-mile north from the main campground, are perched on scenic wooded bluffs above the lake. Check out one of the five hiking trails available at the park, including the 11-mile-long Chief Illini Trail.

65 Wolf Creek State Park

Location: About 25 miles southeast of Decatur
Season: All year except Dec
Sites: 304 sites with electrical hookups, 78 sites with no hookups
Maximum length: 40 feet
Facilities: Flush toilets, water, tables, grills, dump station, showers, beach, hiking trails, playground, boat launch
Fee per night: $–$$$

Management: Illinois Department of Natural Resources
Contact: (217) 459-2831; http://dnr.state.il.us/lands/landmgt/parks/r3/wolfcrek.htm; reservations accepted
Finding the campground: Head south from Decatur on US 51. Go left on CR 1200 North in Assumption. After passing through Findlay, turn right on Wolf Creek Road, which leads into the park.
UTM coordinates: 16S, 354955 E, 4370898 N
About the campground: Located on one of the many scenic, wooded peninsulas on Lake Shelbyville, this sprawling campground seems to have an endless number of sites. The camping area is mostly shaded, flat, and fringed by attractive oak-hickory woods. Other parts of the park feature picnicking spots set within savanna and prairie on the shore of the lake. The park contains an elaborate trail system, including long snowmobile and equestrian trails.

66 Lone Point Recreation Area

Location: About 30 miles southeast of Decatur
Season: May 3 to beginning of Sept
Sites: 91 sites with electrical hookups, 7 sites with no hookups
Maximum length: 40 feet
Facilities: Flush toilets, water, tables, grills, showers, dump station, amphitheater, hiking trail, boat ramp, dock, fish-cleaning station, playground, pay telephone
Fee per night: $$
Management: U.S. Army Corps of Engineers
Contact: (217) 774-3951; www.mvs.usace.army.mil/Shelbyville/recreate.htm; www.recreation .gov or (877) 444-6777 for reservations
Finding the campground: Head south from Decatur on US 51. Go left on CR 1200 North in Assumption. In Findlay, go right on CR 2100 East. Turn left on CR 1800 North and then turn right on CR 2150 East. Turn left on CR 1725 East and then turn right CR 2175 East. Signs will lead you much of the way.
UTM coordinates: 16S, 351387 E, 4369891 N
About the campground: Throughout this campground, scenic views of Lake Shelbyville and its wooded shores peek through the oak and hickory trees. The campsites, situated on gently rolling terrain, tend to be shaded and well spaced. Catch the Chief Illini Trail near the boat launch. It takes you through woodland and prairie along the shore of Lake Shelbyville for 11 miles to Eagle Creek State Park.

67 Coon Creek Recreation Area

Location: About 25 miles southeast of Decatur
Season: Beginning of Apr to end of Oct
Sites: 224 sites with electrical hookups, 8 sites with water and electrical hookups
Maximum length: 45 feet

Facilities: Flush toilets, water, tables, grills, dump station, amphitheater, beach, boat ramp, basketball court, dock, fish-cleaning station, laundry, hiking trail, playground, showers, pay telephone
Fee per night: $$
Management: U.S. Army Corps of Engineers
Contact: (217) 774-3951; www.mvs.usace.army.mil/Shelbyville/recreate.htm; (877) 444-6777 or www.recreation.gov for reservations
Finding the campground: Head south from Decatur on US 51. Go left on CR 1200 North in Assumption. Turn right in Findlay on CR 2100 East. Turn right on CR 1800 North; then turn left on CR 2075 East.
UTM coordinates: 16S, 348780 E, 4368401
About the campground: Like all Lake Shelbyville campgrounds, this one caters heavily to the RVing set. This mostly shaded campground features rolling terrain and a number of attractive shoreline camping options. Its large size and extra amenities—such as a beach—make this campground especially popular on summer weekends. You'll see a variety of trees, flowers, and ferns, as well as a lookout tower, on the campground's hiking trail.

68 Lithia Springs Recreation Area

Location: About 5 miles north of Shelbyville
Season: Beginning of Apr to the end of Oct
Sites: 115 sites with electrical hookups, 8 sites with electrical and water hookups
Maximum length: 40 feet
Facilities: Flush toilets, water, tables, grills, dump station, showers, playground, boat launch, picnicking areas, swimming beach, fish-cleaning station, laundry facilities, amphitheater
Fee per night: $$
Management: U.S. Army Corps of Engineers
Contact: (217) 774-3951; www.mvs.usace.army.mil/Shelbyville/recreate.htm; www.recreation .gov or (877) 444-6777 for reservations
Finding the campground: From I-57, head west on IL 16. Before entering Shelbyville, turn right on CR 2200 East. Turn left on CR 1500 North.
UTM coordinates: 16S, 348434 E, 4366226 N
About the campground: Lithia Springs is the southernmost campground on Lake Shelbyville, the third-largest lake in the state. The campsites are well spaced and mostly open. Some spots sit right on the water and many are located next to small ravines. A full-service marina is located adjacent to the campground. On the way into Shelbyville, the 110 foot high dam offers excellent views of Lake Shelbyville and its wooded shores.

69 Hidden Springs State Forest

Location: About 10 miles northwest of Effingham
Season: Year-round

Sites: 25 sites with no hookups
Maximum length: 40 feet
Facilities: Flush toilets, water, tables, grills, dump station, hiking trails, fishing ponds, playground, picnicking areas
Fee per night: $
Management: Illinois Department of Natural Resources
Contact: (217) 644-3091; http://dnr.state.il.us/lands/Landmgt/parks/r3/hsforest.htm
Finding the campground: From Shelbyville, follow CR 6 south. Turn left on CR 800 North (Clarksburg Road). Turn right on CR 2500 East, and right again on CR 700 North. From I-57 near Effingham, head north on IL 32. Turn left on CR 7.
UTM coordinates: 16S, 354146 E, 4353066 N
About the campground: Hidden Springs State Forest offers a tranquil alternative to the bustling Lake Shelbyville campgrounds 10 miles to the north. This rustic park is sprinkled with pine plantations, scenic ponds, and dense woodland and is bisected by Richland Creek. Half of the campground sits in an open grassy area; the other half sits within woodland fringed by a series of small ravines. A couple of interpretive nature trails will introduce you to the great variety of oaks, maples, hickories and sycamore trees within the forest.

From Springfield to the South

	Hookup Sites	Total Sites	Max RV Length	Hookups	Toilets	Showers	Drinking Water	Dump Station	Recreation	Fee	Reservations
70 Vandalia Lake	25	25	40	E	F	Y	Y	Y	F, L, S	$$	N
71 Ramsey Lake State Recreation Area	90	135	45	E	F	Y	Y	Y	F, H, L	$$	Y
72 Sherwood Forest	200	275	40	E	F	Y	Y	Y	F, L, S	$$	N
73 Lake Lou Yeager	24	24	40	E, W	F	Y	Y	Y	F, H, L, S	$$$	Y
74 Beaver Dam Lake State Park	66	84	40	E, W	F	Y	Y	Y	H, F, L	$$	N
75 Rives Lake	61	61	35	E, W	F	Y	Y	Y	H, F	$$	N
76 White Hall Recreational Park	20	20	40	E, W	F	N	Y	Y	F	$$	N
77 Roodhouse Community Park	34	34	45	E, S, W	F	Y	Y	Y	F	$$	N
78 Lake Jacksonville	12	12	45	E	F	Y	Y	Y	F, L	$$$	N
79 Sangchris Lake State Park: Deer Run	80	130	45	E	NF	N	Y	Y	F, H, L, R	$-$$	N
80 Sangchris Lake State Park: Hickory Point	55	65	45	E	F	Y	Y	Y	F, H, L	$-$$	Y
81 Illinois State Fairgrounds	300	800	50	E, W	F	Y	Y	Y		$$$	N
82 Riverside Park	67	87	40	E, W	F	Y	Y	Y	H	$$	N
83 Lincoln's New Salem State Park	100	200	45	E	F	Y	Y	Y	H	$$-$$$	N
84 Jim Edgar Panther Creek State Fish and Wildlife Area	84	138	40	E, S, W	F	Y	Y	Y	F, H, L, R, C	$$	N

70 Vandalia Lake

Location: 30 miles west of Effingham
Season: Beginning of Apr to mid-Oct
Sites: 25 sites with electrical hookups
Maximum length: 40 foot
Facilities: Flush toilets, showers, grills, water, tables, dump station, beach, beach house, volleyball court, picnic shelters, marina, playground
Fee per night: $$
Management: City of Vandalia
Contact: (618) 283-4770
Finding the campground: From I-70 in Vandalia, take exit 61 and head east on US 40. Turn left on IL 185. Turn right on CR 575 East and follow signs for the campground.
UTM coordinates: 16S, 314104 E, 4319913 N
About the campground: Vandalia Lake offers a nice spot to spend a lazy afternoon casting a line from the shore. This clean, well-maintained municipal park contains a collection of open camp-

sites on the shore of a 660-acre lake. Many campers dock their boats right at their campsite. Stands of hardwood and pine offer some shade. In addition to lakeside sites, camping also is allowed in the park's open grassy areas.

71 Ramsey Lake State Recreation Area

Location: 30 miles west of Effingham
Season: Year-round
Sites: 90 sites with electrical hookups, 45 sites with no hookups, 7 cabins; wheelchair-accessible sites available
Maximum length: 45 feet
Facilities: Flush toilets, showers, grills, water, tables, dump station, picnic shelter, playground, showers, cabins, boat launch and rentals, hiking trails, concessions
Fee per night: $$
Management: Illinois Department of Natural Resources
Contact: (618) 423-2215; http://dnr.state.il.us/lands/landmgt/parks/r5/ramsey.htm; reservations accepted

Wooded bluffs surround an attractive lake at Ramsey Lake State Recreation Area.

Finding the campground: From I-55 south of Springfield, head east on IL 104. Turn right on IL 29 in Taylorville. In Pana, head south on US 51 for about 10 miles. Turn right on Ramsey Lake Road and follow signs into the park.

UTM coordinates: 16S, 315740 E, 4336337 N

About the campground: Once a place where people would come for fox hunting, this rugged terrain laden with oak and hickory trees now contains a scenic lake and a park. Small ravines run along the edges of the two campgrounds. White Oak Campground offers hookup sites perched on the edge of a knoll above Ramsey Lake; campers can follow stairs down to the dam and spillway. Hickory Grove Campground, containing basic sites, also overlooks the lake. The park road around the lake offers a handful of picnicking spots in secluded areas set up on knolls above the lake. No gas motors are allowed on Ramsey Lake.

72 Sherwood Forest

Location: 40 miles south of Springfield
Season: Apr 1 to Oct 15
Sites: 200 sites with electrical hookups, 75 sites with no hookups
Maximum length: 40 feet
Facilities: Flush toilets, showers, grills, water, tables, dump station, laundry, beach, boat launch
Fee per night: $$
Management: Hillsboro Park District
Contact: (217) 532-5211
Finding the campground: From I-55, head east on IL 16 through Litchfield. In Hillsboro, turn left on East Seward Avenue. Circle the courthouse square, and then turn right (north) on North Main Street. After North Main Street turns into North Road, turn right on Glenn Shoals Drive. At Lake Drive Street, turn left.
UTM coordinates: 16S, 286759 E, 4339422 N
About the campground: This campground occupies mostly flat woodland above Lake Hillsboro. The central campground is dominated by a fleet of seasonally parked RVs. Shooting off from the central area, the outer camping areas (named in accordance with the Robin Hood theme) are in wooded areas somewhat tucked away from the hubbub. Some of the sites are located on a 60-foot knoll above small inlets on the one-hundred-acre lake that was constructed in 1918. A nearby swimming beach entices visitors for a dip in the lake. A few more basic sites are offered near the picnic area closer to the dam.

73 Lake Lou Yeager

Location: About 40 miles south of Springfield
Season: Beginning of Apr to end of Oct
Sites: 24 sites with water and electrical hookups
Maximum length: 40 feet

Facilities: Flush toilets, showers, grills, water, tables, dump station, boat launch, marina, beach, picnic areas

Fee per night: $$$

Management: City of Litchfield

Contact: (217) 324-4771; www.cityoflitchfieldil.com/news/28-1.html; reservations accepted

Finding the campground: From I-55 south of Springfield, head east on IL 16. Pass through Litchfield, and then turn left on Yeager Lake Trail. Follow signs to the campground.

UTM coordinates: 16S, 274339 E, 4341763 N

About the campground: The camping area within this 300-acre park is bordered by densely wooded ravines. Campsites are open but well shaded; some require a short walk for access. The park is loaded with picnic areas, playgrounds, a marina, and a beach with shower houses. The 1,200-acre lake has no horsepower limit or speed-limit restrictions. After fishing the stocked waters at Lake Lou Yeager, consider a trip to the Sky-View Drive-in Theater on historic Route 66 in nearby Litchfield.

74 Beaver Dam Lake State Park

Location: About 40 miles from both Springfield and St. Louis, Missouri

Season: Year-round

Sites: 66 sites with water and electrical hookups, 18 sites with no hookups; wheelchair-accessible sites available

Maximum length: 40 feet

Facilities: Flush toilets, showers, grills, water, tables, dump station, cabin, playground, picnic areas, restaurant, concessionaire, boat launch, fish-cleaning station, hiking trails

Fee per night: $$

Management: Illinois Department of Natural Resources

Contact: (217) 854-8020; http://dnr.state.il.us/lands/landmgt/parks/r4/beaver.htm

Finding the campground: From I-55 south of Springfield, take IL 108 west. In Carlinville, turn left on Alton Road (at the Amtrak station). Alton Road eventually becomes Shipman Road. The entrance to the park is on the right. Coming from the south on I-55, follow IL 16 west. On the west side of Shipman, take Carlinville Road (CR 6) to the park.

UTM coordinates: 16S, 242986 E, 4344527 N

About the campground: Both of the camping areas at this park—one with hookups, one without—are flat and mostly open. Stands of oak and hickory offer ample shade. Both campgrounds are a short walk from the lake and the park restaurant; each is situated near agricultural land that borders the park. The campground with amenities is fringed by attractive wooded ravines. A collection of hiking trails crisscross the park and circle the lake.

A wooden walkway at Beaver Dam State Park zigzags through bottomland woods.

75 Rives Lake

Location: About 45 miles southwest of Springfield
Season: Beginning of Apr to the end of Oct
Sites: 61 sites with water and electrical hookups
Maximum length: 35 feet
Facilities: Flush toilets, showers, grills, water, tables, dump station, fishing dock, picnic area
Fee per night: $$
Management: City of Greenfield
Contact: (217) 368-2338
Finding the campground: From I-55 south of Springfield, head west on IL 108. Turn right on IL 267. Turn right on Chestnut Street in Greenfield and keep to the right as the road turns into CR 1600 North. Turn right on CR 2225 East and follow signs to the campground.
UTM coordinates: 15S, 741994 E, 4358227 N

The Rives Lake Campground sits on the lake's rolling shoreline.

About the campground: This quiet campground is located on a little reservoir just outside of the small rural town of Greenfield. What the campsites lack in privacy, they make up for in visual charm. The compact campground is set on a grassy, shaded hill that slopes down to the water. Local anglers use the nearby boat launch.

76 White Hall Recreational Park

Location: About 20 miles south of Jacksonville
Season: Beginning of Apr to end of Oct
Sites: 20 sites (2 wheelchair-accessible) with water and electrical hookups
Maximum length: 40 feet
Facilities: Flush toilets, water, grills, tables, dump station
Fee per night: $$
Management: City of White Hall
Contact: (217) 374-2345
Finding the campground: From I-72 south of Jacksonville, head south on US 67 for about 20 miles. In White Hall, turn left on East Lincoln Street (CR 9). The entrance to the park is on the left.
UTM coordinates: 15S, 725184 E, 4368940 N
About the campground: Located just outside the small community of White Hall, this campground is situated on the grassy shore of a reservoir within a small community park. This low-key, newly built campground is bordered by ball fields, patches of woodland, and agricultural land.

77 Roodhouse Community Park

Location: About 15 miles south of Jacksonville
Season: Beginning of Apr to end of Oct
Sites: 22 sites with water and electrical hookups; 12 sites with water, electrical, and sewer hookups
Maximum length: 45 feet
Facilities: Flush toilets, showers, grills, water, tables, dump station, playground, performance stage
Fee per night: $$
Management: City of Roodhouse
Contact: (217) 589-5374
Finding the campground: From I-72 south of Jacksonville, head south on US 67 for about 15 miles. South of Roodhouse, turn left on CR 2400 North. The entrance to the park is on the right.
UTM coordinates: 15S, 726817 E, 4371448 N
About the campground: This campground is located alongside a small lake within an active eighty-acre community park. The tightly clustered sites in the main camping area offer views of the lake, but no shade. A few sites along the dam on the south side of the lake offer more privacy and shade. During the summer, the park shows films at the outdoor performance stage. Campers are close to the shore of the small lake where they can cast a fishing line.

78 Lake Jacksonville

Location: Several miles south of Jacksonville
Season: Mid-Apr to mid-Oct
Sites: 12 sites with electrical hookups
Maximum length: 45 feet
Facilities: Flush toilets, showers, grills, water, tables, dump station, boat launch, concessionaire
Fee per night: $$$
Management: City of Jacksonville
Contact: (800) 593-5678
Finding the campground: From I-72 south of Jacksonville, head south on IL 67. Turn left on New Lake Road.
UTM coordinates: 15S, 740568 E, 4395622 N
About the campground: The Lake Jacksonville campground occupies a series of little fingers of land that reach out into a 500-acre lake. Most of the campground is dominated by seasonally parked RVs. Drop-in campers are invited to use section 5, which is grassy and unshaded; and section 8, which offers wooded sites next to the water. The bustling park is well loved by local anglers and those seeking refuge from nearby Jacksonville.

79 Sangchris Lake State Park: Deer Run

Location: 15 miles southeast of Springfield
Season: Apr to mid-Jan
Sites: 80 sites with electrical hookups, 40 sites with no hookups, 5 walk-in sites, 5 equestrian sites, 7 wheelchair-accessible sites
Maximum length: 45 feet
Facilities: Vault toilets, water, grills, tables, dump station, play lot, boat launch (showers available at nearby Hickory Point Campground)
Fee per night: $-$$
Management: Illinois Department of Natural Resources
Contact: (217) 498-9208; http://dnr.state.il.us/lands/landmgt/parks/r4/sangch.htm
Finding the campground: From I-55 south of Springfield, follow exit 96A (IL 29) southeast to Rochester. Turn right on Cardinal Hill Road in Rochester. Turn left on New City Road and follow signs to the park and the Deer Run Campground.
UTM coordinates: 16S, 288292 E, 4391864 N
About the campground: This large, flat, and grassy camping area is shaded by attractive specimens of oak, hickory, and sycamore trees. Those who prefer privacy can head to the adjoining walk-in camping area. Trailheads for the hiking and equestrian trails that crisscross this part of the park are easy to find. The best hike starts at the walk-in camping area and takes you down along the lush wooded banks of Clear Creek, where you'll encounter groves of towering cottonwood trees, a variety of waterbirds, and, if you're lucky, one of the albino deer that live in park. Hickory Point Campground, also in the park, is located on the shore of the Sangchris Lake.

80 Sangchris Lake State Park: Hickory Point

Location: 15 miles southeast of Springfield
Season: Apr to mid Jan
Sites: 55 sites with electrical hookups, 10 sites with no hookups, several wheelchair-accessible sites, 2 small cabins
Maximum length: 45 feet
Facilities: Flush toilets, water, grills, showers, tables, dump station, play lot
Fee per night: $-$$
Management: Illinois Department of Natural Resources
Contact: (217) 498-9208; http://dnr.state.il.us/lands/landmgt/parks/r4/sangch.htm; reservations accepted
Finding the campground: From I-55 south of Springfield, follow exit 96A (IL 29) southeast to Rochester. Turn right on Cardinal Hill Road in Rochester. Turn left on New City Road and follow signs to the park and the Hickory Point Campground.
UTM coordinates: 16S, 288991 E, 4390666 N
About the campground: It's no surprise that this campground reels in the anglers. They come for the fishing docks within the camping area, the close proximity of the boat launch and fish-cleaning station, and the many fishing-friendly campsites with grassy banks situated right on the shore of Sangchris Lake. For all these reasons—as well as its showers—Hickory Point is the busier of the park's two campgrounds. The lake allows boats with motors of 25 horsepower or less.

81 Illinois State Fairgrounds

Location: The northern edge of Springfield
Season: Beginning of Apr to the beginning of Oct
Sites: 300 sites with water and electrical hookups, 500 sites with no hookups; wheelchair-accessible sites available
Maximum length: 50 feet
Facilities: Flush toilets, showers, grills, water, tables, dump station
Fee per night: $$$
Management: Illinois State Fair
Contact: (217) 782-1698; www.agr.state.il.us/spacerental/facility/comp.php
Finding the campground: From I-55 in Springfield, head west on Sangamon Avenue (exit 100B). Enter the fairgrounds on the right at Gate 11 (8th Street) or Gate 10.
UTM coordinates: 16S, 273848 E, 4412252 N
About the campground: This RV-oriented campground offers a seemingly endless number of side-by-side campsites. The camping area is flat and minimally shaded; it's located in the southwest corner of the sprawling fairgrounds, near the multipurpose arena and the Agri-Expo. One of the largest state fairs in the Midwest opens on the grounds in mid-Aug.

82 Riverside Park

Location: The northern edge of Springfield
Season: Mid-May to mid-Oct
Sites: 13 sites with water, sewer, and electrical hookups; 54 sites with water and electrical hookups; 20 sites with no hookups
Maximum length: 40 feet
Facilities: Flush toilets, grills, showers, water, tables, dump station, picnic shelter, BMX track, hiking trails
Fee per night: $$
Management: Springfield Park District
Contact: (217) 753-0630 or (217) 544-1751
Finding the campground: From I-55 on the northeast side of Springfield, head west on IL 54. Turn right on Peoria Road. Turn left into the campground before the BMX track.
UTM coordinates: 16S, 275618 E, 4414730 N
About the campground: The west side of the park is bordered by the snaking Sangamon River and thick bottomland woods sprinkled with oxbow ponds. Residential and commercial areas also border the park, as does a busy thoroughfare. The sites, partially shaded, sit fairly close together; tent campers have more room to spread out.

83 Lincoln's New Salem State Park

Location: 15 miles northwest of Springfield
Season: Year-round
Sites: 100 sites with electrical hookups, 100 sites with no hookups
Maximum length: 45 feet
Facilities: Flush toilets, showers, grills, water, tables, dump station, picnic shelters, historic village, outdoor theater, gift shop, concessionaire, restaurant
Fee per night: $$–$$$
Management: Illinois Department of Natural Resources
Contact: (217) 632-4000; www.lincolnsnewsalem.com
Finding the campground: From I-55 north of Springfield, head west on Dinius Road (CR 2) from the Williamsville exit. Continue straight ahead on IL 124. Turn right on IL 29, then turn left on IL 123. Stay on IL 123 heading south from Petersburg. Signs along the highway will point you to the campground.
UTM coordinates: 16S, 257024 E, 4429349 N
About the campground: This campground is part of a park that contains a re-creation of the rural village where Lincoln spent his early adulthood. The side-by-side campsites in the main camping area fill up quickly on desirable weekends. The tent camping area has a gently rolling topography. Both camping areas are very open with minimal shade. The centerpiece of the park is the restored village where Lincoln clerked in a store, split rails, served as postmaster and deputy surveyor, and finally was elected to a state government post.

84 Jim Edgar Panther Creek State Fish and Wildlife Area

Location: 25 miles northwest of Springfield

Season: Year-round

Sites: 19 sites with water, electrical, and sewer hookups; 65 sites with electrical hookups; 9 primitive rental cabins; 51 equestrian sites with electrical hookups; 7 hike-in campsites; wheelchair-accessible sites available

Maximum length: 40 feet

Facilities: Flush toilets, showers, grills, water, tables, dump station, picnic shelter, fishing and boat dock, boat launch, hiking and mountain biking trails

Fee per night: $$

Management: Illinois Department of Natural Resources

Contact: (217) 452-7741; http://dnr.state.il.us/lands/landmgt/parks/r4/jepc.htm

Finding the campground: From I-55 north of Springfield, head south on the South Sherman Boulevard/Veterans Parkway exit. Turn right on IL 97. Continue west on IL 125 as IL 97 turns to the right. Just west of Ashland turn right on Newmansville Road and follow the signs into the park.

UTM coordinates: 15S, 750662 E, 4431212 N

About the campground: Many of the campsites in this enormous state park offer views of Prairie Lake and its wooded shores. The camping area, which sits on a small rise above the lake, is flat and lightly shaded. Campers have ready access to fishing docks and a boat launch, as well as many miles of hiking, biking, and equestrian trails within the park. The park was bought in the early 1990s from a company that abandoned plans to mine coal from the area and build a coal-fired power plant. The park comprises large swaths of prairie and cropland and also a generous amount of rolling wooded terrain.

Between the Rivers

The two major rivers that border west-central Illinois—the Mississippi and the Illinois—cemented Illinois' and Chicago's status as a transportation epicenter. In the twenty-first century, barge traffic continues to chug up and down these rivers, reminding us of the role they still play in the midwestern economy.

But the rivers are far more than just industrial transportation routes. Their expansive wetlands and wooded bluffs create prime recreation spots. When the Illinois River turns south after passing LaSalle and Peru, it grows wide and flows through sprawling wetlands and backwater eddies. Indeed, from Peoria south, the Illinois River becomes the Everglades of the prairie. Many of these cattail marshes, algae-covered ponds, and lakes blanketed in lily pads have been set aside as state and federal land—primarily for use by hunters and anglers.

Continuing south to where the Illinois River meets up with the Mississippi River, you'll encounter Pere Marquette State Park, one of the most scenic parks in Illinois. At the top of its soaring river bluffs, a series of viewing platforms overlook the confluence of three great rivers—the Illinois, the Mississippi, and the Missouri—and barely visible in the distance, is the Arch of St. Louis.

Heading back north along the Mississippi brings you through a series of river towns, strung like beads on a string. As these towns sprang up alongside the Great River, the spotlight glimmered on them for a while. Now, these off-the-beaten-path towns are fascinating to visit: River transport has changed, but the charming ambience of these communities remains. All the towns possess boat launches, and many have municipal riverside campgrounds, usually under the shade of cottonwoods.

Getting closer to the Quad Cites brings you through Nauvoo, a small Mississippi River town founded by the Mormons in the early days of the church. Across the road from Nauvoo State Park sits a collection of buildings from the mid-1800s that was associated with the church and its founder, Joseph Smith. The town is situated in a beautiful spot on a hill overlooking a wide bend in the Mississippi.

While rivers take center stage in this part of the state, there is plenty of dry land to explore, too. A handful of good-sized state parks will keep you busy for many days with rugged hiking, fishing, horseback riding, paddling, and just kicking up your feet at your campsite with a pair of field glasses and a birding guidebook.

The Illinois River: South of Peoria

		Hookup Sites	Total Sites	Max RV Length	Hookups	Toilets	Showers	Drinking Water	Dump Station	Recreation	Fee	Reservations
85	Anderson Lake Fish and Wildlife Area	0	100	45	N/A	NF	N	Y	Y	F, L	$	N
86	Havana Riverfront Park	12	12	35	E, W	F	N	Y	Y	F, L	$$	Y
87	Fulton County Camping and Recreation Area	18	43	45	E	F	Y	Y	Y	F, L	$$	N
88	Canton Lake Campground	68	82	45	E, W	NF	N	Y	Y	F, L, S	$$	N
89	Rice Lake State Fish and Wildlife Area	36	36	45	E	NF	N	Y	Y	F, L	$$	Y
90	Sand Ridge State Forest	0	39	40	N/A	NF	N	Y	Y	H, R	$	N
91	Spring Lake State Fish and Wildlife Area	0	70	40	N/A	NF	N	Y	Y	F, L	$	N

85 Anderson Lake Fish and Wildlife Area

Location: About 45 miles northwest of Springfield
Season: Year-round
Sites: 100 sites with no hookups
Maximum length: 45
Facilities: Vault toilets, water, tables, grills, dump station, boat launch, picnicking area
Fee per night: $
Management: Illinois Department of Natural Resources
Contact: (309) 759-4484; http://dnr.state.il.us/lands/Landmgt/parks/r1/anderson.htm
Finding the campground: From I-155 south of Peoria, head west on US 136, passing through Havana. At IL 100, turn left and proceed nearly 9 miles until reaching the campground on the left.
UTM coordinates: 15T, 738100 E, 4453157 N
About the campground: Squeezed between the Illinois River bluffs and a 1,134-acre lake, this campground offers visitors an attractive place to spend the night. Since the camping area is stretched along the shore of Anderson Lake, many sites are located near the shoreline and nearly all have lake views. The open camping area is shaded with cottonwood and maple. Formerly a private hunting ground, the camping area still attracts hunters as the migratory waterfowl pass through. With a boat launch, a dock, and close access to the Illinois River, anglers love the spot as well. The lake floods occasionally; call ahead to make sure the campground is open.

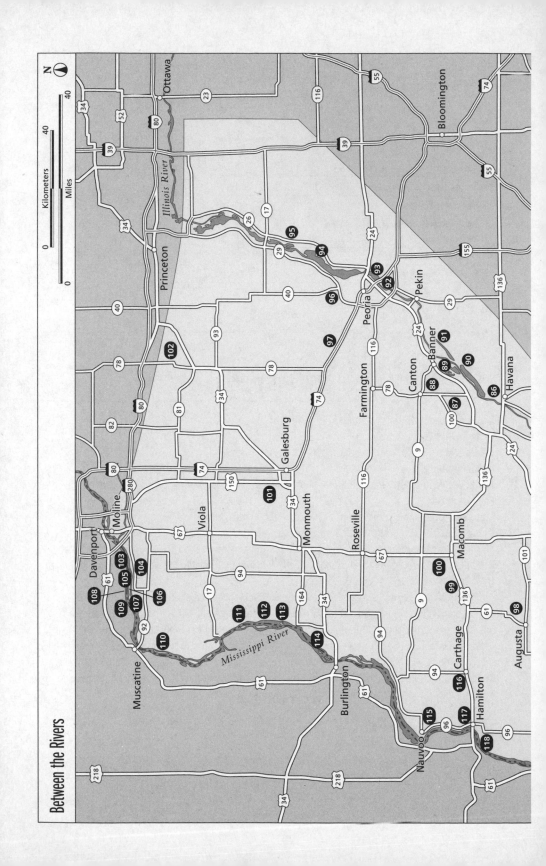

Between the Rivers

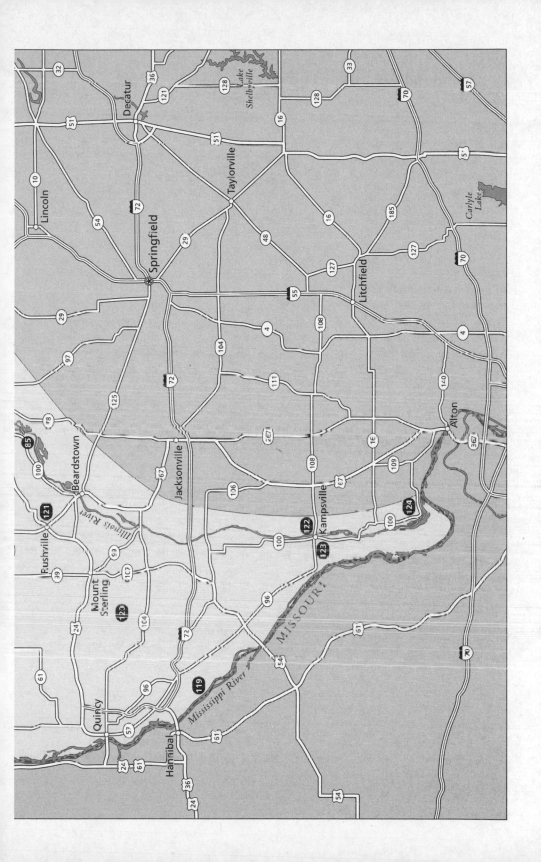

86 Havana Riverfront Park

Location: About 45 miles southwest of Peoria
Season: Year-round
Sites: 12 sites with water and electrical hookups
Maximum length: 35 feet
Facilities: Flush toilets, water, tables, grills, dump station, boat launch, picnic areas
Fee per night: $$
Management: Havana Park District
Contact: (309) 543-6240; www.havana.lib.il.us/community/parkdistrict.html; reservations accepted
Finding the campground: From I-155 south of Peoria, head west on US 136. In Havana, turn right on South Water Street. Head into the park on the left and follow the park road to the campground.
UTM coordinates: 15T, 749380 E, 4465396 N
About the campground: Located between Havana's Riverfront Park and a small marina, this postage-stamp-sized village campground is just blocks from the brick streets and vintage storefronts of downtown Havana. Around the corner from the campground is another park, which has a municipal pool and one of the largest Indian mounds in central Illinois. Havana is a good home base for visiting places such the Dickson Mounds State Museum and the Chautauqua National Wildlife Refuge.

87 Fulton County Camping and Recreation Area

Location: About 35 miles southwest of Peoria
Season: Year-round
Sites: 18 sites with electrical hookups, 25 sites with no hookups
Maximum length: 45 feet
Facilities: Flush toilets, showers, water, tables, grills, dump station, picnic area, playground, boat launch
Fee per night: $$
Management: Fulton County
Contact: (309) 668-2931
Finding the campground: From Peoria, follow US 24 southwest. About 12 miles after Banner, turn right on IL 78. Turn left on the Oscar Linn Highway. Turn right on North Conservation Road. The entrance is on the right.
UTM coordinates: 15T, 747828 E, 4483901 N
About the campground: Once a strip mine and now a county park, this 440-acre camping and recreation area hosts a spaghetti bowl of long, narrow, curving lakes. The myriad scenic ponds, sloughs, and lakes draw anglers and a variety of waterbirds. Little Sister Lake (the only natural lake in the park) and Lake 3 ½ offer pleasant wooded lakeside camping areas off the main park road. Some parts of the park are overflowing with seasonally and permanently parked RVs.

88 Canton Lake Campground

Location: 25 miles southwest of Peoria
Season: Mid-Apr to mid-Oct
Sites: 68 sites with electrical and water hookups, 14 tent sites with no hookups
Maximum length: 45 feet
Facilities: Vault toilets, water, tables, grills, dump station, boat launch, beach
Fee per night: $$
Management: City of Canton
Contact: (309) 647-9600
Finding the campground: From Peoria, take IL 116 west to Farmington. Turn left on IL 78 and proceed into Canton. In Canton, turn left on East Chestnut Street and continue ahead as it jogs left a couple of times. Turn left at the spillway onto North Lakeshore Drive.
UTM coordinates: 15T, 247536 E, 4494840 N
About the campground: This rambling park offers many outstanding views of Canton Lake's hilly, wooded shoreline. The campground is located atop one of the tree-clad bluffs above the 250-acre lake. The 2-mile park road is enjoyable as it snakes up and down the steep banks, through ravines, and past fishing and picnicking areas along the way. Boaters will find solace in the scenic environment of Canton Lake, and paddlers will enjoy a visit to Copperas Creek, accessible from the west end of the lake.

89 Rice Lake State Fish and Wildlife Area

Location: About 25 miles southwest of Peoria
Season: Year-round
Sites: 36 sites with electrical hookups; handicapped-accessible sites available
Maximum length: 45 feet
Facilities: Vault toilets, water, tables, grills, dump station, boat launch, picnic area, fishing dock
Fee per night: $$
Management: Illinois Department of Natural Resources
Contact: (309) 647-9184; http://dnr.state.il.us/lands/Landmgt/parks/r1/rice.htm
Finding the campground: From I-74 in Peoria, take US 24 south toward Lewistown. A few miles after Banner, the entrance to the campground is on the left.
UTM coordinates: 16T, 250094 E, 4484731 N
About the campground: Rice Lake is one of a handful of large bottomland lakes in this central portion of the Illinois River Valley. Located at the shore of Rice Lake, this compact campground has an open layout and is surrounded by dense bottomland woods. Campers come to enjoy the wildlife viewing, as well as fishing and duck hunting. They also use Rice Lake as a home base to visit other nearby natural areas. Just north of Rice Lake is the Banner Marsh State Fish and Wildlife Area, which includes 200 plus bodies of water within some 4,500 acres of marshland.

90 Sand Ridge State Forest

Location: About 30 miles southwest of Peoria
Season: Year-round
Sites: 27 sites with no hookups (1 wheelchair-accessible), 12 backpacking sites
Maximum length: 40 feet
Facilities: Pit toilets, water, tables, grills, dump station, picnic area
Fee per night: $
Management: Illinois Department of Natural Resources
Contact: (309) 597-2212; http://dnr.state.il.us/lands/landmgt/parks/r4/sand.htm
Finding the campground: From I-155 south of Peoria, head west for 20 miles on US 136. Turn right on CR 2800. After Forest City, turn left on East CR 2300 North and continue ahead until reaching the campground on the left.
UTM coordinates: 16T, 256634 E, 4474835 N
About the campground: This little used campground is situated within one of the many pine plantations that grow in Illinois' largest state forest. The pine trees provide for plenty of shade within the camping area. Keep watch for prickly pear cacti, which thrive in the sandy soils of the 7,500-acre state forest. A dozen backcountry primitive campsites are located along more than 40 miles of hiking/equestrian trails. North of the campground, the Jake Wolf Memorial Fish Hatchery has exhibits focusing on fish production at the hatchery, antique fishing tackle, and the Illinois River at the turn of the nineteenth century. Tours are offered every day.

91 Spring Lake State Fish and Wildlife Area

Location: About 25 miles southwest of Peoria
Season: Year-round
Sites: 60 sites with no hookups, 10 walk-in sites
Maximum length: 40 feet
Facilities: Pit toilets, water, tables, grills, dump station, several boat launches, small playground, picnicking areas
Fee per night: $
Management: Illinois Department of Natural Resources
Contact: (309) 968-7135; http://dnr.state.il.us/lands/Landmgt/parks/r1/spl.htm
Finding the campground: Heading south from Pekin on IL 29, turn right on East Manito Road (CR 16). Turn right on Spring Lake Road (CR 21). The entrance to the main camping area is on the right.
UTM coordinates: 16T, 259091 E, 4483224 N
About the campground: This out-of-the-way campground near Spring Lake and the Illinois River is quiet and scenic. The gently rolling terrain is covered with hardwoods and a pine plantation. The sites are fairly spacious and mostly shaded. A handful of campsites tucked away at the edges offer some amount of privacy. Hiking trails are accessible right from the camping area. Down the bluff at Spring Lake, follow the park road for 3 miles as it hugs the shoreline and gives up great views all around—acres of lily pads and water lilies, clusters of waterfowl and wading birds, and wooded bluffs rising above the opposite shore.

The Illinois River: Starved Rock to Peoria

	Hookup Sites	Total Sites	Max RV Length	Hookups	Toilets	Showers	Drinking Water	Dump Station	Recreation	Fee	Reservations
92 Fort Crevecoeur	12	12	40	E, W	NF	N	Y	Y	H	$$	N
93 Carl Spindler Campground and Marina	74	74	40	E, S, W	F	Y	Y	Y	B, H, F, L	$$	N
94 Woodford State Fish and Wildlife Area	0	30	40	N/A	NF	N	Y	Y	F, L	$	N
95 Marshall State Fish and Wildlife Area	22	28	40	E	NF	N	Y	Y	H, F, L	$-$$	N
96 Kickapoo Creek Recreation Area	0	10	N/A	N/A	NF	N	Y	N	C, H	$	N
97 Jubilee College State Park	107	133	40	E	F	Y	Y	Y	C, H	$-$$	N

92 Fort Crevecoeur

Location: Across the Illinois River from Peoria
Season: Beginning of Apr to beginning of Nov
Sites: 12 sites with water and electrical hookups
Maximum length: 40 feet
Facilities: Vault toilets, water, tables, grills, dump station, historic fort, gift shop/museum
Fee per night: $$
Management: Fort Crevecoeur, Inc.
Contact: (309) 694-3193; www.ftcrevecoeur.org
Finding the campground: From East Peoria, head south on IL 29 into Creve Coeur. Turn right on Lawnridge Drive and look for the park entrance on the left.
UTM coordinates: 16T, 279840 E, 4502874 N
About the campground: Located on a bluff overlooking the Illinois River, Fort Crevecoeur commemorates French explorer Robert Rene Cavalier de LaSalle's presence here in 1680. The campground—located in a residential part of Creve Coeur—is set in an open grassy field surrounded by hardwoods. On the north side of the park, a replica of LaSalle's fort has been reconstructed to its original dimensions and design. A nature trail leads hikers through a thickly wooded ravine.

93 Carl Spindler Campground and Marina

Location: Across the Illinois River from Peoria
Season: Beginning of Mar to beginning of Dec
Sites: 48 sites with water, sewer, and electrical hookups, 26 sites with electrical hookups
Maximum length: 40 feet
Facilities: Flush toilets, water, tables, grills, showers, laundry, dump station, marina, boat launch, store, picnic shelter, canoe and kayak rentals, beach

Fee per night: $$
Management: Fondulac Park District
Contact: (309) 699-3549; http://fondulacpark.com/spindlermarina.html
Finding the campground: From I-74 in Peoria, head east over the Illinois River. Exit at US 150/IL 116 and go north. Follow the signs to the Spindler Marina and turn left on Access Road 7 (Marina Lane).
UTM coordinates: 16T, 285550 E, 4509643 N
About the campground: This campground provides easy access to the Illinois River and Peoria—as well as the casino down the road. Campsites are cheek-to-jowl except for the tent sites, which occupy a string of prime spots along the shore of the river. The shoreline offers views of Peoria across the Illinois River, which swells to a width of a mile at this point. From the marina, you can explore the River Trail as it runs south for 2 miles along the river.

94 Woodford State Fish and Wildlife Area

Location: About 20 miles north of Peoria
Season: Beginning of Apr to end of Oct
Sites: 30 sites with no hookups
Maximum length: 40 feet
Facilities: Vault toilets, water, tables, grills, dump station, fishing channels, fish-cleaning station, boat ramp, picnic area
Fee per night: $
Management: Illinois Department of Natural Resources
Contact: (309) 822-8861; http://dnr.state.il.us/lands/Landmgt/parks/r1/woodford.htm
Finding the campground: From East Peoria, take IL 116 north to IL 26. Turn left on IL 26. The park entrance is on the left.
UTM coordinates: 16T, 293464 E, 4528001 N
About the campground: Situated on a spit of bottomland that reaches out into one of the Illinois River's large pools, this camping area is an angler's paradise. No boat is needed to fish the 0.5 mile of constructed fishing channels that are fed by artesian wells. The partially shaded campground is located in a large open area fringed with cottonwood, silver maple, and willow. The pool, known as Goose Lake, is a favorite stopping point for waterfowl during migration. The campground floods periodically; call ahead to check on conditions before you visit.

95 Marshall State Fish and Wildlife Area

Location: About 25 miles north of Peoria
Season: Year-round
Sites: 22 sites with electrical hookups, 6 sites with no hookups
Maximum length: 40 feet
Facilities: Vault toilets, water, tables, grills, dump station, boat launch, fishing channel
Fee per night: $–$$

Management: Illinois Department of Natural Resources

Contact: (309) 246-8351; http://dnr.state.il.us/lands/Landmgt/parks/r1/marshall.htm

Finding the campground: From I-74 in Peoria, take IL 116 north to IL 26. Turn left on IL 26. The park entrance is on the left after passing the Woodford State Fish and Wildlife Area.

UTM coordinates: 16T, 295583 E, 4536359 N

About the campground: The appeal of this campground is its location right on Babb Slough, one of the many bottomland lakes that accompany the Illinois River in the middle of the state. Located next to an active highway, this campground is compact in size and partially shaded. The 6,000-acre state fish and wildlife area hosts many wading birds and waterfowl. Needless to say, the campground fills up during waterfowl hunting season. Canoe campers with permits are invited to camp on the islands in the river. Immediately east of the campground, oak- and hickory-clad river bluffs rise up. Trails on the bluffs take hikers into the deep ravines. The north end of the campground hosts a small day-use picnicking area. The campground often floods in spring; call ahead to check on conditions before you visit.

96 Kickapoo Creek Recreation Area

Location: About 15 miles north of Peoria along the Rock Island State Rail Trail

Season: Year-round

Sites: 10 hike-in or bike-in sites

Maximum length: N/A

Facilities: Vault toilets, water, tables, grills, picnic shelter, hiking trails

Fee per night: $

Management: Illinois Department of Natural Resources

Contact: (309) 695-2228

Finding the campground: On the Rock Island State Trail, the campground is located 2 miles north of Alta and 1.8 miles south of Dunlap (the crushed gravel trail runs from Peoria to Toulon). You can also access the camping area by walking 0.6 mile from the parking lot. To reach the parking area from Peoria, follow War Memorial Drive (US 150) northwest of Peoria. Turn right on IL 91. A few miles ahead, turn right on Fox Road. The parking area is located just past the railroad tracks.

UTM coordinates: 16I, 275876 E, 4524077 N

About the campground: Perhaps one of the best rail-trail camping facilities in the Midwest, Kickapoo Creek Recreation Area is a jackpot for campers looking for a quiet, scenic camping spot. Most of the camping sites are clustered in a lightly shaded savanna; a few sites are tucked away in the wooded fringe. The one-hundred-acre recreation area hosts several miles of trails that wind through woodland, alongside a stream, and through a small but spectacular restored prairie. Just north of the recreation area, the Rock Island Trail spans a 40-foot-high bridge over Kickapoo Creek.

97 Jubilee College State Park

Location: About 15 miles northwest of downtown Peoria
Season: Year-round
Sites: 107 sites with electrical hookups, 26 walk-in sites, 7 wheelchair-accessible sites
Maximum length: 40 feet
Facilities: Flush and vault toilets, water, tables, grills, showers, dump station, hiking and mountain biking trails, picnic shelters
Fee per night: $–$$
Management: Illinois Department of Natural Resources
Contact: (309) 446-3758; http://dnr.state.il.us/lands/Landmgt/parks/r1/jubilee.htm
Finding the campground: From Peoria, head northwest on US 150. Follow the signs.
UTM coordinates: 16T, 263036 E, 4522511 N
About the campground: Jubilee College State Park's proximity to Peoria and its scenic atmosphere make it a popular destination on summer holiday weekends. Large old oaks surround the rolling, grassy camping areas. Hikers, mountain bikers, and cross-country skiers can make use of the extensive trail system within the 3,200-acre park. The western side of the park hosts the Jubilee College Historic Site, a boarding school and seminary that operated from 1840 to 1871. The restored two-story Gothic Revival building has been thoroughly restored by the state.

Galesburg and Macomb Areas

	Hookup Sites	Total Sites	Max RV Length	Hookups	Toilets	Showers	Drinking Water	Dump Station	Recreation	Fee	Reservations
98 Weinberg-King State Fish and Wildlife Area	0	28	35	N/A	NF	N	Y	Y	R	$-$$	N
99 Argyle Lake State Park	110	159	40	E	F	Y	Y	Y	H, F, L, R	$-$$$	Y
100 Spring Lake Park	120	138	40	E	F	Y	Y	Y	B, F, C, L	$-$$	N
101 Lake Storey Park	125	125	40	E, W	F	Y	Y	Y	B, H, F, L, S, C	$$-$$$	N

98 Weinberg-King State Fish and Wildlife Area

Location: 40 miles northeast of Quincy
Season: Year-round
Sites: 28 sites with no hookups; equestrian campsites available
Maximum length: 35 feet
Facilities: Vault toilets, grills, water, tables, dump station, picnic shelter
Fee per night: $-$$
Management: Illinois Department of Natural Resources
Contact: (217) 392-2345; http://dnr.state.il.us/lands/landmgt/parks/r4/weinberg.htm
Finding the campground: On I-74 north of Galesburg, head west on US 34. Turn left on US 67. In Macomb, turn right on US 136. After Tennessee, turn left on IL 61. In Auga, turn left on IL 101. From I-72 to the south, head north on IL 107. In Mount Storling, keep going north on IL 99. At IL 101, turn left. The entrance to the park is on the right.
UTM coordinates: 15T, 678661 E, 4455627 N
About the campground: A fragrant stand of white pine trees grows beside Williams Creek as it winds next to the campground. The campground offers a mix of woods and open grassy areas; across the creek, wooded bluffs rise nearly 100 feet. Oak, hickory, locust, and Osage orange grow on the park's rolling and occasionally steep terrain. In addition to the woods, the fish and wildlife area contains swaths of former cropland that have been returned to prairie.

99 Argyle Lake State Park

Location: 45 miles southwest of Galesburg
Season: Year-round
Sites: 110 sites with electrical hookups, 18 sites with no hookups, 31 tent camping sites
Maximum length: 40 feet

Facilities: Flush toilets, grills, showers, water, tables, dump station, picnic shelter, concessionaire, boat launch, boat rental, restaurant, equestrian and hiking trails
Fee per night: $–$$$
Management: Illinois Department of Natural Resources
Contact: (309) 776-3422; http://dnr.state.il.us/lands/landmgt/parks/r1/argyle.htm; reservations accepted
Finding the campground: From I-74 north of Galesburg, take US 34 west. Turn left on US 67. In Macomb, turn right on US 136. In Colchester, turn right on Coal Road.
UTM coordinates: 15T, 687500 E, 4480430 N
About the campground: The unusually rugged terrain at Argyle Lake State Park allowed the park's 1,700 acres of virgin oak-hickory woods to remain intact. Many of the campsites are perched on 70-foot wooded bluffs above the shore of a ninety-three-acre lake. The sites are open, grassy, and surrounded by dense woodland. Most sites have ample room between them. A dozen hiking trails offer a range of difficulty levels, depending on the terrain.

100 Spring Lake Park

Location: 65 miles west of Peoria, just north of Macomb
Season: Beginning of Apr to the beginning of Nov
Sites: 120 sites with electrical hookups, 18 sites with no hookups
Maximum length: 40 feet
Facilities: Flush toilets, grills, showers, water, tables, dump station, picnic shelter, boat launch, boat rental, bike trails
Fee per night: $–$$
Management: Macomb Park District
Contact: (309) 833-2052; http://parks.macomb.com/spring.html
Finding the campground: From I-474 in Peoria, head west on the Maxwell Connector and then continue west on IL 116. In Roseville, turn left on US 67. Before reaching Macomb, turn right on Spring Lake Road. The park is on the left.
UTM coordinates: 15T, 691822 E, 4485583 N
About the campground: This municipal campground near the shore of a 230-acre lake offers plenty of open, grassy sites. Shade is plentiful; privacy is not. Some sites are occupied by seasonal campers. Mountain bikers can explore a collection trails in the park, and hikers can enjoy the woodland, prairie, and wetland at the nearby Lakeview Nature Center.

101 Lake Storey Park

Location: A few miles north of Galesburg
Season: Mid-Apr to mid-Oct
Sites: 13 sites with water and electrical hookups, 112 sites with electrical hookups
Maximum length: 40 feet
Facilities: Flush toilets, grills, showers, water, tables, dump station, picnic shelter, concessionaire, boat rentals, boat launch, beach, hiking and biking trail
Fee per night: $$–$$$
Management: City of Galesburg
Contact: (309) 345-3623; www.ci.galesburg.il.us/parks/lakestorey.htm
Finding the campground: From I-74 north of Galesburg, head west on US 34. Take US 150 north. Turn left on Storey Road. Enter the camping area on the right.
UTM coordinates: 15T, 719521 E, 4540254 N
About the campground: Families will find much to occupy their time in the vicinity of this campground. From the open, woodland-fringed campground, it's a short walk down a knoll to the shore of the lake. Near the campground are beaches, a recreation facility with multiple swimming pools, a restaurant, and a ferry that takes visitors across the 411-acre lake.

The Mississippi River: Quad Cities South to Nauvoo

	Hookup Sites	Total Sites	Max RV Length	Hookups	Toilets	Showers	Drinking Water	Dump Station	Recreation	Fee	Reservations
102 Johnson-Sauk Trail State Recreation Area	70	95	45	E	F	Y	Y	Y	B, H, F, L	$-$$	N
103 Buffalo Shores	65	65	50	E, W	F	Y	Y	Y	F, L, S	$$	N
104 Andalusia Slough	0	16	40	N/A	NF	N	Y	Y	F, L	$	N
105 Clarks Ferry Recreation Area	45	45	45	E, W	F	Y	Y	Y	F, L	$$	Y
106 Shady Creek	53	53	45	E	F	Y	Y	Y	F, L	$$	Y
107 Loud Thunder Forest Preserve	25	112	40	E	F	Y	Y	Y	F, H, L	$$	N
108 Fairport Recreation Area	45	45	40	E	F	Y	Y	Y	F, L	$$	Y
109 Wildcat Den State Park	0	26	40	N/A	NF	N	Y	Y	H	$$	Y
110 Blanchard Island Recreation Area	0	34	35	N/A	NF	N	Y	Y	F, L	$	N
111 Keithsburg Park	64	64	40	E, W	F	Y	Y	Y	F, L	$$	N
112 Big River State Forest	0	70	40	N/A	F	Y	Y	Y	H, F, L	$$	N
113 Delabar State Park	52	58	40	E	F	Y	Y	Y	H, F, L	$-$$	N
114 Henderson County State Fish and Wildlife Area	0	35	35	N/A	NF	N	Y	Y	F, L	$	N

102 Johnson-Sauk Trail State Recreation Area

Location: 30 miles southeast of the Quad Cities
Season: Year-round
Sites: 70 sites with electrical hookups, 25 walk-in sites
Maximum length: 45 feet
Facilities: Flush toilets, showers, water, grills, tables, dump station, picnic shelter, restaurant, concessionaire, boat launch, boat rental, hiking trails
Fee per night: $-$$
Management: Illinois Department of Natural Resources
Contact: (309) 853-5589; http://dnr.state.il.us/lands/landmgt/parks/r1/johnson.htm
Finding the campground: From I-80, head south on IL 78 through Annawan. The entrance to the park is on the left.
UTM coordinates: 16T, 258007 E, 4578614 N
About the campground: The rolling, wooded grounds of this state park host a couple of enticing camping areas, each a short walk from the fifty-eight-acre lake and the concessionaire. The basic campground occupies a dense pine plantation. Those looking to add voltage to their campout can set up on a grassy rise overlooking a stunning prairie rich with wildflowers and an enormous round barn that sits within the park. The barn, 85 feet in diameter, was built in 1910 and is said to be one of the largest round barns in the country.

103 Buffalo Shores

Location: About 10 miles southwest of the Quad Cities on the Iowa shore of the Mississippi River
Season: Mid-Apr to mid-Nov
Sites: 65 sites with water and electrical hookups
Maximum length: 50 feet
Facilities: Flush toilets, showers, water, grills, tables, dump station, picnic shelter, sandy beach, boat launch, playground, camp store, concrete pads
Fee per night: $$
Management: Scott County Conservation Board
Contact: (563) 328-3281; www.scottcountyiowa.com/conservation/bshores.php
Finding the campground: From I-280 south of Rock Island, head west over the Mississippi River into Iowa. Exit on IA 22 and head southwest toward Muscatine. Look for the campground entrance on the left after passing through Buffalo.
UTM coordinates: 15T, 688296 E, 4591363 N
About the campground: About one-quarter of the sites at this campground are at the edge of an attractive sandy beach on the Mississippi River. Like the other riverside campgrounds on this stretch of IA 22, this one caters mostly to RV owners. The side-by-side campsites offer minimal shade. A swath of woodland separates the campground from nearby IA 22. To the north is the Buffalo Bill Cody Homestead, the boyhood home of the western showman. The village of Buffalo, located 0.5-mile upstream from the campground, contains a convenience store and restaurants.

104 Andalusia Slough

Location: 10 miles southwest of the Quad Cities
Season: Year round
Sites: 16 sites with no hookups
Maximum length: 40 feet
Facilities: Vault toilets, water, tables, grills, dump station, picnic shelter, boat launch
Fee per night: $ (fee charged mid-May to mid-Oct)
Management: U.S. Army Corps of Engineers
Contact: (563) 263-7913
Finding the campground: From I-280 south of Rock Island, head southwest on IL 92. The campground appears on the right 2 miles after passing through Andalusia.
UTM coordinates: 15T, 686421 E, 4589626 N
About the campground: This very basic roadside RV campground is squeezed between IL 92 and the dense bottomland woods along the Mississippi River. The camping area is flat and lightly shaded. Anglers come to fish the waters around the dozens of nearby islands in the river. Just a few miles upstream, the Rock River flows into the Mississippi.

105 Clarks Ferry Recreation Area

Location: About 15 miles southwest of the Quad Cities on the Iowa shore of the Mississippi River
Season: Mid-Apr to mid-Oct
Sites: 45 sites with water and electrical hookups
Maximum length: 45 feet
Facilities: Flush toilets, showers, grills, water, tables, dump station, picnic shelter, playground, boat launch
Fee per night: $$
Management: U.S. Army Corps of Engineers
Contact: (563) 263-7913; www.mvr.usace.army.mil/missriver/Recreation/ClarksFerry.htm; (877) 444-6777 or www.recreation.gov for reservations
Finding the campground: From I-280 south of Rock Island, head west over the Mississippi River into Iowa. Exit on IA 22 and head southwest toward Muscatine. Look for the campground entrance on the left in Montpelier.
UTM coordinates: 15T, 682824 E, 4591690 N
About the campground: Like the other RV-oriented roadside campgrounds on this stretch of the Mississippi River, this campground offers great views of the river's main channel (a series of islands prevents the full view of this mile-wide point in the river). The flat, well-shaded camping area is bordered by private residences within the village of Montpelier. Just to the west, IA 22 mounts a bluff offering commanding views of the river. Captain Benjamin Clark, the campground's namesake, operated one of the only ferries in the area between Illinois and Iowa in the early 1800s.

106 Shady Creek

Location: About 20 miles west of the Quad Cities, on the shore of the Mississippi River in Iowa
Season: Beginning of May to end of Oct
Sites: 53 sites with electrical hookups
Maximum length: 45 feet
Facilities: Flush toilets, showers, water, grills, tables, dump station, picnic shelter, playground, boat launch, concrete pads
Fee per night: $$
Management: U.S. Army Corps of Engineers
Contact: (563) 263-7913; www.mvr.usace.army.mil/missriver/Recreation/ShadyCreek.htm; (877) 444-6777 or www.recreation.gov for reservations
Finding the campground: From I-280 south of Rock Island, head west over the Mississippi River into Iowa. Exit on IA 22 and head southwest toward Muscatine. Look for the campground entrance on the left after the turnoff for Wildcat Den State Park.
UTM coordinates: 15T, 677506 E, 4590357 N
About the campground: A pleasing variety of mature trees offer shade for this RV-oriented campground sandwiched between the Mississippi River and IA 22. The river is eminently visible from most of the side-by-side sites in this generous-sized campground. Beyond the river's main channel, low wooded islands pepper the waterway. Waterbirds loiter in the vicinity.

Campers at Shady Creek Campground are steps away from the shore of the Mississippi River.

107 Loud Thunder Forest Preserve

Location: 15 miles southwest of the Quad Cities
Season: Mid-Apr to the end of Oct
Sites: 25 sites with electrical hookups, 87 sites with no hookups
Maximum length: 40 feet
Facilities: Flush toilets, showers, water, grills, tables, dump station, picnic shelters, boat launch, playground
Fee per night: $$
Management: Rock Island County Forest Preserve District
Contact: (309) 795-1040
Finding the campground: From I-280 southwest of Rock Island, head southwest on IL 92. After IL 92 curves left away from the river, turn right on Loud Thunder Road and follow signs to the camping area.
UTM coordinates: 15T, 681769 E, 4588432 N
About the campground: Most of the campsites are situated near wooded ravines that run down to the shore of Lake George. Fringed by thick woods and stands of shrubs, the campground is

The lake at Loud Thunder Forest Preserve is a favorite spot for local anglers.

grassy and open. A few walk-in sites offer a greater degree of privacy. The bluffs surrounding Lake George lend it a strong scenic appeal. A woodland hiking trail offers big views from a bluff above the Mississippi River.

108 Fairport Recreation Area

Location: About 20 miles west of the Quad Cities, on the shore of the Mississippi River in Iowa
Season: Mid-Apr to mid-Oct
Sites: 45 sites with electrical hookups
Maximum length: 40 feet
Facilities: Flush toilets, showers, water, grills, tables, dump station, picnic shelter, fish-cleaning station, boat launch
Fee per night: $$
Management: Iowa Department of Natural Resources
Contact: (563) 263-4337; www.iowadnr.gov/parks/state_park_list/fairport.html/; reservations accepted

Finding the campground: From I-280 south of Rock Island, head west over the Mississippi River into Iowa. Exit on IA 22 and head southwest toward Muscatine. Look for the campground entrance on the left after passing through Fairport.

UTM coordinates: 15T, 673259 E, 4588566 N

About the campground: Despite the close proximity to IA 22, this is one of the best of the handful of local riverside campgrounds in the area that cater largely to RVs. To the north, bluffs rise nearly 200 feet above the campground, and to the south, the expansiveness of the Mississippi opens before you. Watch cargo boats, recreational speedboaters, and waterbirds go by from your campsite or from one of the wooden swinging benches on the riverbank.

109 Wildcat Den State Park

Location: In Iowa, about 20 miles west of the Quad Cities
Season: Year-round
Sites: 26 sites with no hookups
Maximum length: 40 feet
Facilities: Vault toilets, water, tables, grills, dump station, picnic shelter, hiking trails, historic mill
Fee per night: $$
Management: Iowa Department of Natural Resources
Contact: (563) 263-4337; www.iowadnr.gov/parks/state_park_list/wildcat_den.html; reservations accepted
Finding the campground: From I-280 south of Rock Island, head west over the Mississippi River into Iowa. Exit on IA 22 and head southwest toward Muscatine. After passing through Montpelier, turn right on Wildcat Den Road and follow signs to the campground.
UTM coordinates: 15T, 676574 E, 4592718 N
About the campground: The quiet, compact campground is fringed with stately 100-foot oaks. The open layout offers plenty of shaded sites. From the campground, you can catch hiking trails that run through the park's rugged landscape featuring high bluffs and sandstone formations with evocative names such as Devil's Punch Bowl and Fat Man's Squeeze. Trails also lead to a former schoolhouse and gristmill within the park. The mill, built in 1848, and its picnic area sit alongside the wonderfully scenic Pine Creek.

110 Blanchard Island Recreation Area

Location: 35 miles southwest of the Quad Cities
Season: Mid-May to mid-Oct
Sites: 34 sites with no hookups
Maximum length: 35 feet
Facilities: Vault toilets, water, tables, grills, dump station, boat launch
Fee per night: $
Management: U.S. Army Corps of Engineers

Contact: (563) 263-7913; www.mvr.usace.army.mil/missriver/Recreation/BlanchardIsland.htm; reservations not required

Finding the campground: From I-280 south of Rock Island, head southwest on IL 92. Before crossing the Mississippi River into Muscatine, turn left on 322nd Street West. Turn right on 176th Street Avenue West. The campground is at end of the road.

UTM coordinates: 15T, 662601 E, 4579056 N

About the campground: Blanchard Island Recreation Area offers no-frills camping in a riverside hideaway location. The camping area is flat, open, and grassy; groves of maple trees provide ample shade. Half of the sites are only steps from Blanchard Chute, a secondary channel in the Mississippi River. Anglers come for the prime fishing waters among the wooded islands. If you've brought a boat, use it to explore enormous Blanchard Island (nearly four miles long), which is located across the channel from the campground.

111 Keithsburg Park

Location: In Keithsburg, 40 miles southwest of the Quad Cities
Season: Year-round
Sites: 64 sites with water and electrical hookups
Maximum length: 40 feet
Facilities: Flush toilets, showers, grills, water, tables, dump station, picnic shelter, boat launch, volleyball court
Fee per night: $$
Management: City of Keithsburg
Contact: (309) 374-9070 or (309) 374-2311
Finding the campground: From the Quad Cities area, head south on US 67. In Viola, turn right on IL 17. After passing through Joy, turn left on Seventy-sixth Street. Keep straight ahead as Seventy-Sixth Street turns into Fourth Street in Keithsburg and ends at the campground.
UTM coordinates: 15T, 672708 E, 4551480 N
About the campground: This municipal riverside campground is located a couple of blocks from Keithsburg's tiny downtown area. The open, minimally shaded camping area is mostly covered with a gravel surface. Many campsites are close enough to the Mississippi River to allow campers to dock their boats right at their sites. Boaters can explore the many large islands in this section of the river, as well as the Mark Twain National Wildlife Refuge just north of Keithsburg.

112 Big River State Forest

Location: 45 miles southwest of the Quad Cities
Season: Year-round
Sites: 70 sites with no hookups
Maximum length: 40 feet
Facilities: Flush toilets, showers, grills, water, tables, dump station
Fee per night: $$
Management: Illinois Department of Natural Resources
Contact: (309) 374-2496; http://dnr.state.il.us/lands/landmgt/parks/r1/bigriver.htm
Finding the campground: From Galesburg, follow US 34 west to Monmouth. In Monmouth, take II 164 west to Oquawka. Before reaching Oquawka, turn right on CR 3 (CR 1350 East). After passing the park office, turn left on the first driveway on the left (watch carefully; there are no signs for the campground).
UTM coordinates: 15T, 673463 E, 4546546 N
About the campground: Big River State Forest is full of pine plantations, and the camping area is no exception. Flat, fragrant, and heavily shaded, the camping area sits on a bluff several hundred yards from the Mississippi River. A smaller camping area down by the shore of the river is available depending on the whims of floodwater. Hikers can explore the forest on several miles of trails and many more miles of fire lanes. Within the campground, look for birds such as red-headed woodpeckers and nuthatches; down by the river, you're likely to see herons and egrets.

113 Delabar State Park

Location: 45 miles southwest of the Quad Cities
Season: Year-round
Sites: 52 sites with electrical hookups, 6 walk-in sites
Maximum length: 40 feet
Facilities: Flush toilets, showers, grills, water, tables, dump station, playground, boat launch, picnic shelter
Fee per night: $-$$
Management: Illinois Department of Natural Resources
Contact: (309) 374-2496; http://dnr.state.il.us/lands/landmgt/parks/r1/delabar.htm
Finding the campground: From Galesburg, follow US 34 west to Monmouth. In Monmouth, take IL 164 west to Oquawka. Before reaching Oquawka, turn right on CR 3 (CR 1350 East) The entrance to the park is on the left.
UTM coordinates: 15T, 673355 E, 4536207 N
About the campground: This small, narrow park on the shore of the Mississippi River features a gently rolling landscape dominated by oaks and hickories. The camping areas are quiet, secluded and open; each is just a short walk from the river. Walk-in campsites north and south of the main campground offer varying amounts of shade. Mill Island, nearly 1 mile long, sits close the shore on this stretch of river. In Oquawka, 2 miles south of the park, a monument stands at the place where a circus elephant was buried after getting killed by lightning in 1972.

114 Henderson County State Fish and Wildlife Area

Location: 35 miles west of Galesburg

Season: Year-round

Sites: 35 sites with no hookups

Maximum length: 35 feet

Facilities: Vault toilets, grills, water, tables, dump station, picnic shelter, boat ramp

Fee per night: $

Management: Illinois Department of Natural Resources

Contact: (309) 374-2496; http://dnr.state.il.us/lands/landmgt/parks/r1/henderso.htm

Finding the campground: From I-74 in Galesburg, head west on US 34. A few miles after passing IL 94, turn right on Gladstone Lake Road. The entrance to the park is on the left.

UTM coordinates: 15T, 670050 E, 4523996 N

About the campground: Local anglers like to escape to this small quiet park and its lake in pursuit of bass, bluegill, catfish, and crappie. The camping area is open and grassy; many of the sites are right on the shore of the twenty-seven-acre Gladstone Lake. A steady stream of train traffic uses the railroad tracks along the north shore of the lake.

The Mississippi River: From Nauvoo to the South

	Hookup Sites	Total Sites	Max RV Length	Hookups	Toilets	Showers	Drinking Water	Dump Station	Recreation	Fee	Reservations
115 Nauvoo State Park	75	150	45	E	F	Y	Y	Y	H, F, L	$$	N
116 Carthage Jaycee Park	12	12	40	E	F	Y	Y	Y	S	$$	N
117 Wildcat Springs Park	16	16	40	E	NF	N	Y	Y	S	$$	N
118 Warsaw Riverfront Park	20	20	40	E	NF	N	Y	Y	F, L	$$	N
119 Park-n-Fish	0	6	30	N/A	NF	N	N	N	F	$	N
120 Siloam Springs State Park	98	186	50	E	F	Y	Y	Y	H, F, L, R	$$	N
121 Schuy-Rush Park	100	175	45	E, W	F	Y	Y	Y	H, F, L	$$	N
122 Kampsville Village Park	22	22	40	E, S, W	F	Y	Y	Y	H, F	$$$	N
123 McCulley Heritage Project	0	3	N/A	N/A	NF	N	Y	N	H, F	$	N
124 Pere Marquette State Park	80	115	45	E	F	Y	Y	Y	H	$$-$$$	Y

115 Nauvoo State Park

Location: 45 miles north of Quincy
Season: Year-round
Sites: 75 sites with electrical hookups, 75 sites with no hookups; wheelchair-accessible sites available
Maximum length: 45 feet
Facilities: Flush toilets, showers, grills, water, tables, dump station, picnic shelter, museum, lake, boat launch
Fee per night: $$
Management: Illinois Department of Natural Resources
Contact: (217) 453-2512; http://dnr.state.il.us/lands/landmgt/parks/r4/nauvoo.htm
Finding the campground: From Galesburg, head west on US 34. After Biggsville, turn left on IL 94. Continue straight ahead on IL 90 into Lomax. After passing through downtown Nauvoo, the state park is on the left. From Macomb, head west on US 136. In Hamilton, turn right on IL 96. The park is on the right before entering Nauvoo.
UTM coordinates: 15T, 636851 E, 4489276 N
About the campground: Two pleasant campgrounds combined with rich local history make this state park well worth a visit. The modern campground is flat and blanketed with a pine plantation. The basic campground offers rolling grassy terrain with some sites tucked away on the wooded bluffs above a small lake. The Nauvoo Historical Society, located within the park next to the campground, offers a small taste of the area's fascinating history. A short walk from the campground, you'll find dozens of historic buildings that date from the days when the town was an early Mormon settlement.

116 Carthage Jaycee Park

Location: 40 miles northeast of Quincy
Season: Beginning of Apr to mid-Nov
Sites: 12 sites with electrical hookups
Maximum length: 40 feet
Facilities: Flush toilets, showers, grills, water, tables, dump station, playground, public swimming pool, picnic shelter, public golf course
Fee per night: $$
Management: City of Carthage
Contact: (217) 357-3733
Finding the campground: From Macomb, head west US 136. After passing through Carthage, turn right on East CR 1500 just before US 136 curves to the left (look for a sign marking the park entrance).
UTM coordinates: 15T, 656818 E, 4476408 N
About the campground: Golf enthusiasts will be thrilled with the link-side location of this compact municipal campground. The campground, shaded by stately oaks trees, sits on a small knoll above Carthage Lake's rolling shoreline. In Carthage, visitors will want to see the historic Hancock County Courthouse and the Old Carthage Jail where Joseph Smith, the founder of the Mormon Church, died at the hands of an angry mob in 1844.

117 Wildcat Springs Park

Location: 30 miles north of Quincy
Season: Mid-Mar to the beginning of Nov
Sites: 16 sites with electrical hookups
Maximum length: 40 feet
Facilities: Vault toilets, water, grills, tables, dump station, volleyball court, public pool
Fee per night: $$
Management: City of Hamilton
Contact: (217) 847-3788
Finding the campground: From Macomb, head west on US 136. In Hamilton, turn right on North Seventh Street.
UTM coordinates: 15T, 640315 E, 4473698 N
About the campground: This small campground is located on a grassy hilltop under a heavy oak canopy. The park's open, rolling terrain is bounded by residential areas. Look for the exposed rock along Cheney Creek, which runs through the park. On hot summer days, kids and adults stream into the park's municipal pool adjacent to the campground. A few blocks west at the Mississippi River, the hydroelectric dam sits beside Lock No. 19. Heading north from Hamilton along the River Road, catch fantastic river views from a series of scenic turnouts.

118 Warsaw Riverfront Park

Location: 30 miles north of Quincy
Season: Early spring to late fall
Sites: 20 sites with electrical hookups
Maximum length: 40 feet
Facilities: Portable toilets, water, grills, tables, picnic shelter, dump station
Fee per night: $$
Management: City of Warsaw
Contact: (217) 256-3214
Finding the campground: From I-172 northeast of Quincy, head west on US 24. Turn right on IL 96 and proceed for 24 miles. Turn left on Main Street (Warsaw Gravel Road). At the river, turn left on Water Street. From Macomb to the west, follow US 136 west to Hamilton. In Hamilton, turn left on IL 96. Turn right on Main Street (Warsaw Gravel Road), and turn left at Water Street when you reach the river.
UTM coordinates: 15T, 632021 E, 4468267 N
About the campground: Towering cottonwood trees provide ample shade for this petite municipal campground squeezed between the Mississippi River and swelling river bluffs. The open campsites are steps away from the shore of the river. Boat owners can put in at a nearby boat launch. The compact downtown area of Warsaw, located up the bluff, contains a handful of historic buildings. Stop in at the town's former brewery that now serves as a riverfront restaurant.

119 Park-n-Fish

Location: About 25 miles south of Quincy
Season: Year-round
Sites: 6 sites with no hookups
Maximum length: 30 feet
Facilities: Vault toilets, tables, picnic shelter
Fee per night: $
Management: U.S. Army Corp of Engineers
Contact: (309) 794-5338
Finding the campground: From I-72 10 miles east of the Mississippi River, exit south on IL 96. Turn right on IL 106. Turn left on CR 800 East. Turn right on CR 1800 North. Turn left on Lock and Dam Road. The park is on the right.
UTM coordinates: 15T, 650853 E, 4389410 N
About the campground: This primitive, postage-stamp-sized park is bordered by a levee and the river on one side and farm fields on the other. The unshaded sites at this quiet, out-of-the-way spot are at the foot of the Mississippi River Levee opposite Lock and Dam 22. Anglers come here to cast their lines.

120 Siloam Springs State Park

Location: About 20 miles east of Quincy
Season: Year-round
Sites: 98 sites with electrical hookups, 84 sites with no hookups, 4 backpacking sites
Maximum length: 50 feet
Facilities: Flush toilets, showers, grills, water, tables, dump station, hiking and equestrian trails, concessionaire, lake, boat launch
Fee per night: $$
Management: Illinois Department of Natural Resources
Contact: (217) 894-6205; http://dnr.state.il.us/lands/landmgt/parks/r4/siloamsp.htm
Finding the campground: From I-72, head north on IL 107 through Griggsville. Turn left on IL 104, and then after about 12 miles turn right on East 2873rd Lane. The park entrance is on the right.
UTM coordinates: 15S, 676881 E, 4417532 N
About the campground: This out-of-the-way state park contains rugged topography and lovely wooded terrain. The campground, which sits on a wooded ridge that slopes 100 yards down toward Crabapple Lake, contains a mature oak-hickory forest with a sprinkling of pine trees. (Look for monster oaks that are more then 175 years old.) The crystal-clear, spring-fed lake is considered one of the best bass-fishing destinations in the state. The park once was a resort known for its restorative springs. A dozen or so miles of good hiking trails run through the park; the trails provide options for overnight backpacking.

121 Schuy-Rush Park

Location: About 35 miles northwest of Jacksonville
Season: Year-round
Sites: 100 sites with water and electrical hookups, 75 sites with no hookups
Maximum length: 45 feet
Facilities: Flush toilets, water, showers, tables, grills, dump station, picnic shelters, ball diamond, boat launch and slips, playground
Fee per night: $$
Management: Schuyler County
Contact: (217) 322-6628
Finding the campground: From Rushville, take US 67 south to Park Road. Turn right and follow the signs into the park.
UTM coordinates: 15T, 708750 E, 4439784 N
About the campground: The thick woods, rolling landscape, and scenic 225-acre lake give this county campground plenty of flavor. Most of the campsites occupy the central, open grassy areas. Some sites offer more privacy; these are tucked away in the wooded fringes, in between the hills, and down by the boat launch and boat slips. The wooded banks of Schuy-Rush Lake offer a scenic setting for casting a line.

122 Kampsville Village Park

Location: About 60 miles northwest of St. Louis
Season: Year-round
Sites: 22 sites with water, electrical, and sewer hookups
Maximum length: 40 feet
Facilities: Flush toilets, showers, water, tables, dump station
Fee per night: $$$
Management: Village of Kampsville
Contact: (618) 653-4421
Finding the campground: From I-72 west of Jacksonville, follow IL 100 south to Kampsville. From St. Louis to the south, head north on MO 367 from I-270. In Alton, turn left on IL 100 and follow to Kampsville. In Kampsville, the campground is located on the east side of IL 100 near Marquette Street.
UTM coordinates: 15S, 706209 E, 4352419 N
About the campground: This no-frills municipal campground is located within the tiny village of Kampsville, a quiet river town nestled against the wooded bluffs of the Illinois River. The open, grassy, and lightly shaded camping area is a stone's throw from the mighty Illinois River and the dock for the town's free car ferry. The Center of American Archeology, which features exhibits and displays focusing on the area's rich Native American history, sits next to the campground In a historic storefront. Hike the river bluffs at the nearby McCulley Heritage Project.

123 McCulley Heritage Project

Location: About 60 miles northwest of St. Louis
Season: Year-round
Sites: 3 walk-in sites
Maximum length: N/A
Facilities: Vault toilets, water, fire rings, tables, picnic shelter, hiking trails
Fee per night: $
Management: McCulley Heritage Project
Contact: (618) 653-4687, www.mcoullyheritage.org
Finding the campground: From I-72 west of Jacksonville, follow IL 100 south. South of Kampsville, turn right on Crawford Creek Road. From St. Louis to the south, head north on MO 367 from I-270. In Alton, turn left on IL 100 and follow to Kampsville. Before reaching Kampsville, turn left on Crawford Creek Road. The camping area is on the right near the red barn.
UTM coordinates: 15T, 704266 E, 4350436 N
About the campground: After making the 50-yard walk from the parking lot, you'll encounter a well-shaded camping area surrounded by lush bottomland woods. An old red barn, ponds and wetlands, and a frontier cabin/schoolhouse are situated near the camping area. The park, operated as a private nonprofit organization, features 15 miles of hiking trails, a marshland boardwalk, and scenic overlooks.

A boardwalk allows exploration of the wetlands at the McCulley Heritage Project.

124 Pere Marquette State Park

Location: 35 miles northwest of St. Louis
Season: Year-round
Sites: 80 sites with electrical hookups, 35 sites with no hookups; wheelchair-accessible sites available
Maximum length: 45 feet
Facilities: Flush toilets, showers, grills, water, tables, dump station, hiking trails, lodge, visitor center, restaurant
Fee per night: $$–$$$
Management: Illinois Department of Natural Resources
Contact: (618) 786-3323; http://dnr.state.il.us/lands/landmgt/parks/r4/peremarq.htm; reservations accepted
Finding the campground: From St. Louis, head north on MO 367 from I-270. In Alton, turn left on IL 100. From I-55 to the east, follow IL 140 into Alton. In Alton, keep straight ahead on College Avenue. Turn left on US 67. Turn right on IL 100. After passing through Grafton, the park entrance is on the right.

UTM coordinates: 15T, 713488 E, 4316014 N

About the campground: Pere Marquette State Park claims a position as one of the most scenic—and popular—state parks in Illinois. The large, modern camping area sits in a flat expanse close to IL 100; the basic campground, offering more privacy, is further from the highway and partially set on a bluff. Hardwoods provide ample shade all around. A park visitor center and the impressive park lodge containing a hotel, a restaurant, and a gift shop are a short walk away. Marvel at the 40-mile views of the surrounding rivers, lakes, and floodplains at the top of the park's soaring river bluffs.

The Illinois River and its attending backwater lakes are visible from the top of the soaring bluffs at Pere Marquette State Park.

Southern Illinois

I t's surprising how few Midwesterners are familiar with the breathtaking beauty of the 270,000-acre Shawnee National Forest. The forest occupies a huge swath of rugged terrain at the southern tip of the state, and is bordered by the Ohio River on the east and Mississippi River on the west. As one of the few parts of Illinois to escape the flattening effects of the last glacier, the Shawnee hosts deep canyons, fantastic rock formations, rugged woodland, and frequent waterfalls. Its sandstone cliffs, quiet rocky streams, and high bluffs dotted with wildflowers give it a scenic beauty unparalleled in the state.

Hikers have a huge number of options at Shawnee. Fall is a particularly rewarding season to strap on the hiking boots: Oak, hickory, poplar, sumac, and ash trees guarantee an abundance of color. Oaks produce a rich display of reds and browns; sweet gum can be red, yellow, or purple; shagbark hickory offers golden browns. Some of the best hiking is on the 146-mile River to River Trail (accessible from several campgrounds). Garden of the Gods Recreation Area, Giant City State Park, and Cedar Lake offer trails that are also well worth a visit. In addition to hiking, Shawnee is known for its many miles of equestrian trails. Guides and horse rentals are easy to find.

Many RVers, anglers, and boaters have their sights set a little further north in this region toward the two largest lakes in the state: Carlyle Lake and Rend Lake. These lakes are fringed with attractive woodland containing many hundreds of campsites. In some of these campgrounds, anglers can cast a fishing line right from their campsite. While exploring the many dozens of inlets surrounding these lakes, anglers and wildlife watchers will be pleased with what they find.

From St. Louis to the South

	Hookup Sites	Total Sites	Max RV Length	Hookups	Toilets	Showers	Drinking Water	Dump Station	Recreation	Fee	Reservations
125 Horseshoe Lake State Park	0	48	40	N/A	NF	N	Y	Y	H, F, L	$	N
126 World Shooting and Recreational Complex	1,001	1,001	50	E, S, W	F	Y	Y	Y	F, L	$$-$$$	N
127 Fort Kaskaskia State Historic Site	32	82	40	E	NF	N	Y	Y	H	$-$$	N
128 Randolph State Fish and Wildlife Area	51	131	45	E	F	Y	Y	Y	B, H, F, L	$$-$$$	N
129 Pyramid State Recreation Area	0	41	40	N/A	NF	N	Y	Y	H, F, L	$	N
130 Du Quoin State Fairgrounds	1,000	1,500	50	E, W	F	Y	Y	Y	H, C	$$	N
131 Washington County State Conservation Area	51	151	50	E	F	Y	Y	Y	H, F, L, C	$$-$$$	N

125 Horseshoe Lake State Park

Location: 7 miles west of St. Louis
Season: The beginning of May to the end of Oct
Sites: 48 sites with no hookups
Maximum Length: 40 feet
Facilities: Vault toilets, grills, water, tables, dump station, picnic shelters, boat launch, concessionaire
Fee per night: $
Management: Illinois Department of Natural Resources
Contact: (618) 931-0270; http://dnr.state.il.us/lands/landmgt/parks/r4/horsesp.htm
Finding the campground: From the south, exit I-55/70 on IL 111 heading north. The entrance to the park is on the left. From the north, exit I-255 by heading west on Horseshoe Lake Road. Turn left on IL 111 and enter the park on the right.
UTM coordinates: 15S, 754014 E, 4285407 N
About the campground: The greater part of this 3,000-acre park consists of a large oxbow lake that surrounds an island. The lake was formed by floodwaters from the Mississippi River before local levees were built. The camping areas located on the southern tip of the island— are flat and open with varying amounts of shade. Access the island by following a causeway often lined with anglers. The generous swaths of nearby wetlands will require that you keep the bug spray handy A hiking trail circling the entire the island offers great views of the lake.

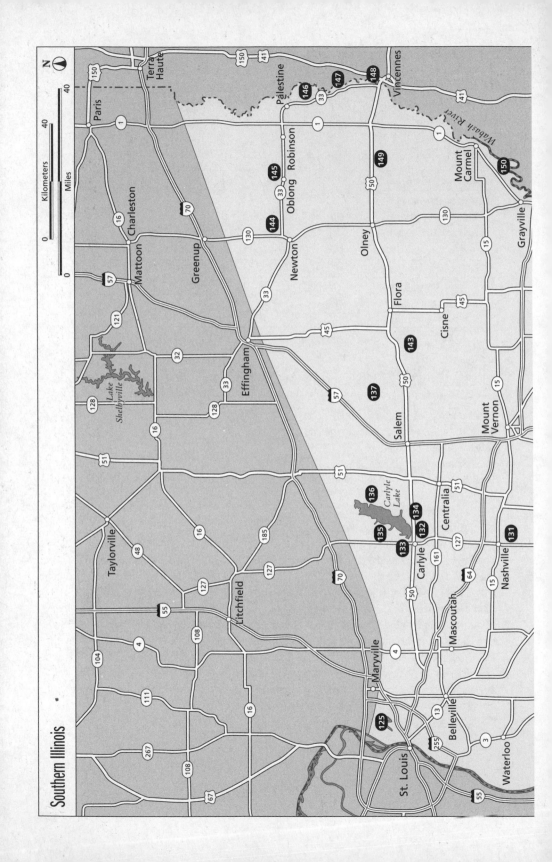

Southern Illinois

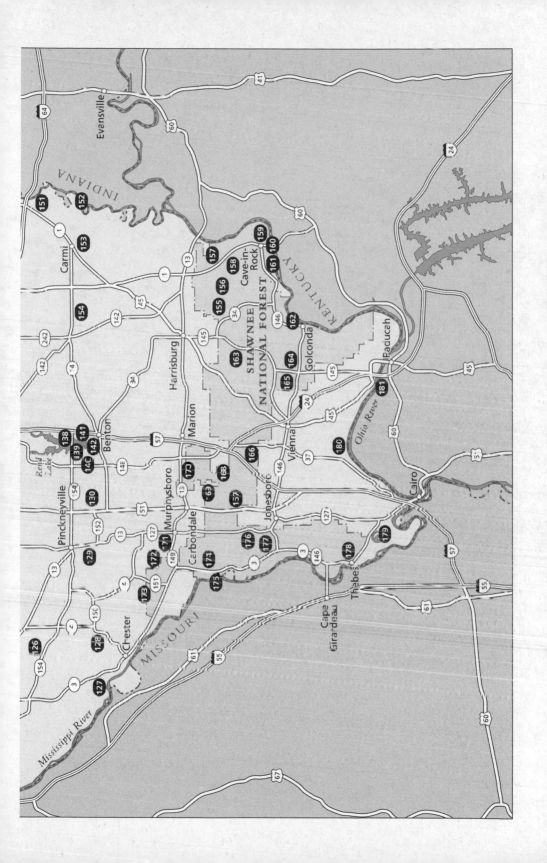

Horseshoe Lake State Park contains a large oxbow lake decorated with water lillies, lily pads, and cattails.

126 World Shooting and Recreational Complex

Location: 45 miles southeast of St. Louis
Season: Year-round
Sites: 341 sites with water, electrical, and sewer hookups; 350 sites with water and electrical hookups; 310 sites with electrical hookups; wheelchair-accessible sites available
Maximum length: 50 feet
Facilities: Flush toilets, showers, grills, water, tables, dump station, recreation hall, picnic shelters, fishing lake, boat launch, playground, restaurant, shooting ranges
Fee per night: $$-$$$
Management: Illinois Department of Natural Resources
Contact: (618) 295-2700; http://dnr.state.il.us/worldshooting/camping.htm
Finding the campground: From I-64 east of St. Louis, head south on IL 4 for about 25 miles. After passing Marissa, turn right on CR 18.
UTM coordinates: 16S, 258068 E, 4230297 N
About the campground: In recent years, the state of Illinois opened this enormous shooting facility on land reclaimed from strip mining. The generous-sized, full-hookup sites are paved while the others are gravel. Most of the sites are situated side by side; some offer larger spaces. Shade is minimal as the newly planted trees grow in size. The facility offers several types of shooting, including skeet, trap, sporting clays, and a cowboy shooting gallery. Anglers have a choice of three lakes to launch boats.

127 Fort Kaskaskia State Historic Site

Location: About 60 miles southeast of St. Louis on the shore of the Mississippi River
Season: Year-round
Sites: 32 sites with electrical hookups, 50 sites with no hookups
Maximum length: 40 feet
Facilities: Tables, grills, vault toilets, water, dump station, picnic shelters
Fee per night: $-$$
Management: Illinois Department of Natural Resources
Contact: (618) 859-3741; www.illinoishistory.gov/hs/fort_kaskaskia.htm
Finding the campground: From I-255 south of St. Louis, head south on IL 3. Drive south for nearly 50 miles. Before reaching Chester, turn right on Shawneetown Trail and follow signs into the park.
UTM coordinates: 16S, 244268 E, 4200630 N
About the campground: Fort Kaskaskia State Historic Site sits on a wooded bluff 200 feet above a big bend in the Mississippi River. The small camping area is open and grassy; pine and maple trees offer ample shade. The historic site commemorates the location of a fort that was intermittently occupied by U.S. and French troops since 1759. The park also is the site of an old cemetery that was moved here in 1891 to avoid the floodwaters in another nearby location. A footpath leads to the Pierre Menard Home State Historic Site, located at the bottom of the bluff. A traditional music festival comes to the park the third weekend in Sept.

Fort Kaskaskia State Historic Site overlooks a big bend in the Mississippi River.

128 Randolph State Fish and Wildlife Area

Location: About 60 miles southeast of St. Louis
Season: Year-round
Sites: 51 sites with electrical hookups, 80 sites with no hookups, 3 wheelchair-accessible sites
Maximum length: 45 feet
Facilities: Tables, grills, flush toilets, showers, water, dump station, playground, picnic shelters, hiking and equestrian trails, boat ramp
Fee per night: $$–$$$
Management: Illinois Department of Natural Resources
Contact: (618) 826-2706; http://dnr.state.il.us/lands/landmgt/parks/r4/rand.htm
Finding the campground: From I-255 south of St. Louis, head south on IL 3. Drive south for nearly 50 miles. Before reaching Chester, turn left on Shawneetown Trail. Turn right on Palestine Road and enter the park on the left. Coming from Chester to the south, turn right on Oak Street while traveling north on IL 3. Turn left on Van Zant Street, and right on Palestine Road. The entrance to the park is on the right.
UTM coordinates: 16S, 253737 E, 4206299 N

About the campground: Visitors at the Randolph State Fish and Wildlife Area have three different campgrounds from which to choose. Two of the campgrounds feature basic sites well shaded by oak trees. Some of these sites require a short walk from the parking area to the shore of the park's sixty-five-acre wooded lake. The main campground, located in a flat area next to the park office, is shady and open. Nearby attractions include the Fort Kaskaskia Historic Site south of the park, St. Mary's Covered Bridge on IL 150, and a statue and small museum in honor of Popeye in Chester (the birthplace of the cartoon character's creator).

129 Pyramid State Recreation Area

Location: About 30 miles northwest of Carbondale
Season: Year-round
Sites: 35 sites with no hookups, 6 hike-in sites
Maximum length: 40 feet
Facilities: Tables, grills, vault toilets, water, dump station, multiple boat ramps, picnicking areas
Fee per night: $
Management: Illinois Department of Natural Resources
Contact: (618) 357-2574; http://dnr.state.il.us/lands/landmgt/parks/r5/pyramid.htm
Finding the campground: From I 57 near Rend Lake, take IL 154 west to US 51. Turn left. In Du Quoin, take IL 152 east. The park entrance is 8 miles ahead on the right. From I-64 to the north, take IL 127 south. Turn right on IL 152.
UTM coordinates: 16S, 287830 E, 4209039 N
About the campground: At nearly 20,000 acres, Pyramid State Recreation Area is the largest state owned natural area. It's also one of two large state parks on land formerly used for strip mining. The remnants of the mining operations at Pyramid are the many ponds ranging from ultra tiny to intermediate in size. The many piles of mine tailings give the landscape a rolling appearance. Take your pick of camping areas: Some spots are set within a cluster of ponds and some are tucked away among a series of rolling mounds. The Heron Campground, however, occupies a relatively undisturbed piece of flat wooded landscape in the southwest corner of the main park area. The many ponds stocked with game fish make Pyramid a favorite spot for anglers.

130 Du Quoin State Fairgrounds

Location: About 20 miles north of Carbondale
Season: Year-round
Sites: 1,000 sites with water and electrical hookups; space for more than 500 tenting sites
Maximum length: 50 feet
Facilities: Tables, grills, flush toilets, showers, water, dump station
Fee per night: $$
Management: Du Quoin State Fair
Contact: (618) 542-1515; www.agr.state.il.us/dq
Finding the campground: From I-57 near Rend Lake, take IL 154 west to US 51. Turn left. In Du Quoin, turn left on Tracy Lane and enter Gate 3. In the off-season, enter through the main gate on IL 51 south of Tracy Lane.
UTM coordinates: 16S, 304246 E, 4206713 N
About the campground: The campsites at Du Quoin State Fairgrounds are clustered near the covered rodeo and alongside one of the fairground's ponds. The sites are positioned closely together and offer little shade. The fairground's many ponds and rolling terrain makes it a great place for strolling and bike riding. Events are held at the fairgrounds during much of the year, but the big show is at the end of Aug when some 400,000 people from all over southern Illinois come to enjoy the fair.

131 Washington County State Conservation Area

Location: About 20 miles west of Rend Lake
Season: Year-round
Sites: 51 sites with electrical hookups, 100 sites with no hookups
Maximum length: 50 feet
Facilities: Tables, grills, flush toilets, showers, water, dump station, boat launch
Fee per night: $$–$$$
Management: Illinois Department of Natural Resources
Contact: (618) 327-3137; www.dnr.state.il.us/lands/landmgt/parks/r4/washco.htm
Finding the campground: About 50 miles east of St. Louis, exit I-64 and head south on IL 127. The park will appear on the left several miles after passing through Nashville. Coming from Pinckneyville to the south, head north on IL 127. Look for the entrance on the right.
UTM coordinates: 16S, 293626 E, 4239317 N
About the campground: It's understandable why this small park has a loyal following on the weekends. The picturesque 160-acre lake and the small bluffs laden with oak trees provide a peaceful refuge. The campsites—many of which are situated near the shore of the lake—are open and shaded. A few of the basic campsites require a short walk from the parking area. Consider dropping in at the Black Diamond Winery located across IL 127, or several miles up the road in Nashville, visit the Washington County Historical Museum.

Carlyle Lake Area

	Hookup Sites	Total Sites	Max RV Length	Hookups	Toilets	Showers	Drinking Water	Dump Station	Recreation	Fee	Reservations
132 Dam East Spillway	10	15	40	E	NF	N	Y	N	F	$$	Y
133 Dam West	113	113	50	E, S, W	F	Y	Y	Y	F, L, S	$$	Y
134 McNair	36	44	35	E	F	Y	Y	Y	H, F, S	$$	Y
135 Eldon Hazlet State Park	328	364	50	E	F	Y	Y	Y	H, F, L, S	$$-$$$	Y
136 Boulder Access Area	74	84	50	E	F	Y	Y	Y	F, L	$$-$$$	Y
137 Stephen Forbes State Park	117	131	45	E	F	Y	Y	Y	H, F, L, R	$-$$$	N

132 Dam East Spillway

Location: 0.5-mile northeast of Carlyle at the Carlyle Lake spillway
Season: Year-round
Sites: 10 sites with electrical hookups, 5 sites with no hookups
Maximum length: 40 feet
Facilities: Tables, grills, vault toilets, water, fish-cleaning station, picnic shelter, playground, dam
Fee per night: $$
Management: U.S. Army Corps of Engineers
Contact: (618) 594-2484; www.mvs.usace.army.mil/carlyle; (877) 444-6777 or www.recreation .gov for reservations
Finding the campground: From the St. Louis area, head east on I-64. Exit I-64 at US 50 and continue heading east. After passing through Carlyle, turn left on the Dam East access road and stay to the left until reaching the campground on the back side of the dam.
UTM coordinates: 16S, 295652 E, 4276408 N
About the campground: What this campground lacks in size, it makes up for in drama. Positioned next to the 70-foot-high Carlyle Dam spillway, this camping spot attracts anglers who fish the waters of the Kaskaskia River and people who enjoy the sight of millions of gallons of rushing water. The campground is flat and open with little shade. South Shore State Park 1 mile to the east offers one of the quieter places to retreat to along the shore of the massive Carlyle Lake.

133 Dam West

Location: 1 mile north of Carlyle on the west shore of Carlyle Lake
Season: Beginning of Apr to beginning of Nov
Sites: 28 sites with electric, water, and sewer hookups; 85 sites with only electrical hookups; 1 wheelchair-accessible site
Maximum length: 50 feet
Facilities: Tables, grills, flush toilets, showers, water, dump station, laundry, marina, amphitheater, beach, playground
Fee per night: $$
Management: US Army Corps of Engineers
Contact: (618) 594-2484; www.mvs.usace.army.mil/carlyle; (877) 444-6777 or www.recreation .gov for reservations
Finding the campground: From the St. Louis area, head east on I-64. Exit I-64 at US 50 and continue heading east. In Carlyle, head north on IL 127. Turn right on CR 20. The main entrance is on the right.
UTM coordinates: 16S, 294804 E, 4278297 N
About the campground: Nestled between a marina and a golf course, this campground offers a resortlike atmosphere on the shore of Carlyle Lake. The 26,000-acre lake is one of the most popular RV camping areas in the state. Sites are well shaded with cypress, sycamore, and oak trees. Many sites are close to the water overlooking dozens of sailboats moored at the marina. This campground offers quick access to the beach, the visitor center, and the hiking trails at the Dam West Recreation Area.

134 McNair

Location: 1 mile northeast of Carlyle on the south shore of Carlyle Lake
Season: Beginning of May to end of Sept
Sites: 36 sites with electrical hookups, 8 sites with no hookups
Maximum length: 35 feet
Facilities: Tables, grills, flush toilets, showers, water, dump station, beach, picnic shelters
Fee per night: $$
Management: U.S. Army Corps of Engineers
Contact: (618) 594-2484; www.mvs.usace.army.mil/carlyle; (877) 444-6777 or www.recreation .gov for reservations
Finding the campground: From the St. Louis area, head east on I-64. Exit I-64 at US 50 and continue heading east. After passing through Carlyle, turn left on the Dam East entrance road and continue straight ahead through the four-way stop sign and proceed into the McNair group area.
UTM coordinates: 16S, 298392 E, 4276479 N
About the campground: While the signs identify McNair as a group campground, individuals are also welcome to set up camp. The campground occupies a gently rolling wooded shoreline just east of Carlyle Lake's 1.25-mile-long earthen dam. Campsites are semisheltered; some sites are close to the water. The campground's northern shore contains riprap, while the eastern shore hosts

a sandy beach that looks toward South Shore State Park. Anglers can cast from the bank or use the fishing dock.

135 Eldon Hazlet State Park

Location: 6 miles north of Carlyle on the west shore of Carlyle Lake
Season: Year-round
Sites: 328 sites with electrical hookups, 36 walk-in sites, wheelchair-accessible sites available
Maximum length: 50 feet
Facilities: Tables, grills, flush toilets, showers, water, dump station, campground store, swimming pool, hiking trails, boat launch, playground
Fee per night: $$–$$$
Management: Illinois Department of Natural Resources
Contact: (618) 594-3015; www.dnr.state.il.us/lands/landmgt/parks/r4/eldon.htm; reservations accepted
Finding the campground: From the St. Louis area, head east on I-64. Exit I-64 and continue heading east US 50. In Carlyle turn left on IL 127. Follow signs heading into the park on the right. Coming from I-70 to the north, exit south on IL 127. Follow signs heading into the park to the left.
UTM coordinates: 16S, 297547 E, 4281722 N
About the campground: This huge campground takes up 1.5 miles of the western shore of Carlyle Lake, the largest human-made lake in the state. Virtually all of the campsites are within 100 yards of the shore, and many sites are perched on a small bluff overlooking the 3-mile-wide lake (some campers are able to cast a fishing line from their sites). The camping areas are flat and well shaded with hickory and maple trees. The park offers a number of amenities, such as a grocery store and swimming pool.

136 Boulder Access Area

Location: 14 miles northeast of Carlyle on the east shore of Carlyle Lake
Season: Mid-Apr to mid-Sept
Sites: 74 sites with electrical hookups, 10 sites with no hookups
Maximum length: 50 feet
Facilities: Tables, grills, flush toilets, water, picnic shelter, playground, amphitheater, boat ramp, showers, beach, dump station, laundry facility, marina, fishing docks
Fee per night: $$–$$$
Management: U.S. Army Corps of Engineers
Contact: (618) 594-2484; www.mvs.usace.army.mil/carlyle; (877) 444-6777 or www.recreation .gov for reservations
Finding the campground: From the St. Louis area, head east on I-64. Exit I-64 at US 50 and continue heading east. After passing through Carlyle, turn left on CR 3 (CR 2500 East). The entrance to the campground is on the left. From US 51 to the east, head west on CR 1300 North. After CR 1300 North turns into CR 1700 North, turn right on CR 3 (CR 2550 East).

UTM coordinates: 16S, 305371 E, 4284920 N

About the campground: This out-of-the-way campground sits on a gently rolling peninsula within a fragrant grove of pine trees. Some of the campsites overlook a wetland area connected to Carlyle Lake. Other sites are nestled against the lake's shoreline and offer excellent views of the surrounding wooded shores. Walk-in sites occupy a finger of land surrounded by the lake.

137 Stephen Forbes State Park

Location: 25 miles east of Carlyle Lake
Season: Year-round
Sites: 117 sites with electrical hookups, 4 sites with no hookups, 10 walk-in sites
Maximum length: 45 feet
Facilities: Tables, grills, flush toilets, showers, water, dump station, boat launch, beach, marina, restaurant, playground, picnic shelters, equestrian and hiking trails, equestrian campground
Fee per night: $–$$$
Management: Illinois Department of Natural Resources
Contact: (618) 547-3381; http://dnr.state.il.us/lands/landmgt/parks/r5/stephen.htm
Finding the campground: From I-57 south of Effingham, exit heading east on CR 8 to Kinmundy. Turn left on IL 37. From Kinmundy, follow signs to the park. From US 50 to the south, head north on Omega Road, which leads into the park.
UTM coordinates: 16S, 346792 E, 4286978 N
About the campground: This large state park features an ample camping area on a northern crook of a big artificial lake. A series of small ravines border the well-shaded camping area. The isolated tent camping area is flat and heavily wooded with hickory trees. Good fishing waters combined with a marina and a restaurant attract anglers from throughout the area. Picnicking areas are spread out along the lake's many arms.

Rend Lake Area

	Hookup Sites	Total Sites	Max RV Length	Hookups	Toilets	Showers	Drinking Water	Dump Station	Recreation	Fee	Reservations
138 Wayne Fitzgerrell State Park	243	283	45	E	F	Y	Y	Y	H, F, L, C, B	$-$$$	N
139 North Sandusky Recreation Area	105	118	45	E, S, W	F	Y	Y	Y	F, L, C	$$	Y
140 South Sandusky Recreation Area	119	127	45	E, W	F	Y	Y	Y	F, L	$$	Y
141 Gun Creek	100	100	45	E	F	Y	Y	Y	F, L	$$	Y
142 South Markham Recreation Area	147	161	45	E	F	Y	Y	Y	H, F, L	$$	Y

138 Wayne Fitzgerrell State Park

Location: 10 miles south of Mount Vernon on the east shore of Rend Lake
Season: Year-round
Sites: 243 sites with electrical hookups, 40 walk-in sites, 8 wheelchair-accessible sites
Maximum length: 45 feet
Facilities: Tables, grills, flush and vault toilets, showers, picnicking shelters, water, boat launch, dump station, hiking and bicycle trails, lakeside resort with restaurant, marina, various lodging options
Fee per night: $-$$$
Management: Illinois Department of Natural Resources
Contact: (618) 629-2320, http://dnr.state.il.us/lands/landmgt/parks/r5/wayne.htm
Finding the campground: On I-57 south of Mount Vernon, exit on IL 154 and head west. After crossing an arm of Rend Lake, the entrance to the park is on the right.
UTM coordinates: 16S, 330391 E, 4219787 N
About the campground: One could get lost within the many loops and cul-de-sacs that fill this park's main campground. Sites extend out on a series of flat, wooded peninsulas into Rend Lake. The tent camping area at the north end of the park offers plenty of shade for sites spread out along the shore of the lake. Privacy is limited at both campgrounds. A 4-mile hiking/biking trail winds through the park's wooded and wetland areas The park's resort offers two different dining options.

139 North Sandusky Recreation Area

Location: 25 miles south of Mount Vernon on the west side of Rend Lake
Season: Beginning of Apr to end of Oct
Sites: 105 sites with electrical hookups; 13 sites with electrical, water, and sewer hookups; 7 wheelchair-accessible sites
Maximum length: 45 feet

Facilities: Tables, grills, flush toilets, showers, water, dump station, boat ramp, picnic shelters, playgrounds
Fee per night: $$
Management: U.S. Army Corps of Engineers, St. Louis District
Contact: (618) 724-2493; www.mvs.usace.army.mil/rend/; (877) 444-6777 or www.recreation .gov for reservations
Finding the campground: On I-57 south of Mount Vernon, head west on IL 154. After crossing Rend Lake, turn right on North Sandusky Creek Drive.
UTM coordinates: 16S, 324975 E, 4215185 N
About the campground: The campsites at the North Sandusky Recreation Area are clustered around one of Rend Lake's many tree-fringed inlets. The wooded campsites are lined up on a series of cul-de-sacs and loops that slope gradually down to the shore of the lake. A bicycle trail runs from this campground all the way to the Rend Lake visitor center. Rend Lake was created in the early 1970s in part to relieve the scarcity of water in this part of the state.

140 South Sandusky Recreation Area

Location: 25 miles south of Mount Vernon on the west side of Rend Lake
Season: Beginning of Apr to end of Oct
Sites: 111 sites with electrical hookups, 8 sites with electrical and water hookups, 8 tent camping sites, several wheelchair-accessible sites
Maximum length: 45 feet
Facilities: Tables, grills, flush toilets, showers, water, dump station, boat ramp, picnic shelters, playgrounds
Fee per night: $$
Management: U.S. Army Corps of Engineers, St. Louis District
Contact: (618) 724-2493; www.mvs.usace.army.mil/rend/; (877) 444-6777 or www.recreation .gov for reservations
Finding the campground: On I-57 south of Mount Vernon, head west on IL 154. After crossing Rend Lake, turn left on North Sandusky Creek Drive. Turn right on Rend City Road and follow it as it curves left. The entrance is on the left.
UTM coordinates: 16S, 324637 E, 4214091 N
About the campground: Compared to its sister campground immediately to the north, the South Sandusky Campground features terrain a bit more rolling and wooded. Fewer of these sites sit next to the water, and more are located within areas densely wooded with pine and maple. The Syca-more section offers sites that are widely spaced and tucked away in the woods. This campground is a short walk from the Rend Lake Marina, which contains a prime picnicking spot and a beach.

141 Gun Creek

Location: The east shore of Rend Lake, about 20 miles south of Mount Vernon
Season: Beginning of Apr to end of Oct

Sites: 100 sites with electrical hookups
Maximum length: 45 feet
Facilities: Tables, grills, flush toilets, showers, water, dump station, boat ramp, picnic shelters, amphitheater
Fee per night: $$
Management: U.S. Army Corps of Engineers, St. Louis District
Contact: (618) 724-2493; www.mvs.usace.army.mil/rend/; (877) 444-6777 or www.recreation.gov for reservations
Finding the campground: From I-57 south of Mount Vernon, head west on IL 154. Turn left on Gun Creek Trail, and then turn right on Golf Course Road.
UTM coordinates: 16S, 330625 E, 4216368 N
About the campground: This campground provides a convenient location to make use of the dining room and the greens at the nearby Rend Lake Golf Course. Like the other Rend Lake camping options, this campground leans strongly toward RV users. Many of the campsites sit on wooded banks that slope down gradually toward Rend Lake. Maple, oak, and tulip trees provide shade. Nearby, at Gun Creek Trail and IL 154, the Southern Illinois Artisans Shop and Art Gallery features excellent art exhibitions, as well as an impressive collection of arts and crafts made by Illinois folks.

142 South Markham Recreation Area

Location: 8 miles north of Benton on the south shore of Rend Lake
Season: Beginning of Apr to beginning of Nov
Sites: 147 sites with electrical hookups, 14 tenting sites
Maximum length: 45 feet
Facilities: Tables, grills, flush toilets, showers, water, dump station, boat ramp, picnic shelters, playgrounds, hiking trail
Fee per night: $$
Management: U.S. Army Corps of Engineers, St. Louis District
Contact: (618) 724-2493; www.mvs.usace.army.mil/rend/; (877) 444-6777 or www.recreation.gov for reservations
Finding the campground: From I-57 south of Mount Vernon, exit on IL 14 heading east. Quickly turn right on North Central Street. North Central Street becomes Rend Lake Road and then becomes Mine 24 Road. The campground entrance is on the right before crossing the Rend Lake Dam.
UTM coordinates: 16S, 330063 E, 4211214 N
About the campground: This attractive campground features gently rolling terrain, groves of pine trees, and a small pond with a hiking trail around it. The campsites are well shaded and mostly open. Many sit on grassy banks above Rend Lake, and some occupy 50-foot bluffs overlooking the lake. RVs are the main focus here, but there is also a collection of walk-in tent camping sites on a peninsula that juts out into the lake. The campground is within walking distance of the dam, which provides top-notch views of the 18,900-acre lake.

East Side and the Wabash River

	Hookup Sites	Total Sites	Max RV Length	Hookups	Toilets	Showers	Drinking Water	Dump Station	Recreation	Fee	Reservations
143 Sam Dale State Fish and Wildlife Area	70	88	40	E	NF	N	Y	Y	H, F, L	$-$$	Y
144 Sam Parr State Park	32	67	45	E, W	NF	N	Y	Y	H, F, L, R	$-$$	N
145 Oblong Park and Lake	10	10	45	E	F	Y	Y	Y	H	$$	N
146 Leaverton Park	400	500	45	E, W	F	Y	Y	Y	H	$$	Y
147 Ouabache Trails Park	35	44	40	E, W	F	Y	Y	Y	H	$$	N
148 Kimmell Park	0	25	40	N/A	F	Y	Y	N	H, L	$-$$	N
149 Red Hills State Park	100	120	40	E	F	Y	Y	Y	H, R	$-$$$	N
150 Beall Woods State Park	0	16	30	N/A	NF	N	Y	N	H, F	$	N
151 Hilltop	20	20	40	E, W	F	Y	Y	Y	L, S	$$	N
152 Harmonie State Park	200	200	40	E	F	Y	Y	Y	C, H, F, L, R	$$-$$$	Y
153 Burrell Park	20	45	45	E, S, W	F	Y	Y	N	H, F	$-$$	N
154 Hamilton County State Fish and Wildlife Area	60	60	40	E	F	Y	Y	Y	F, H, L	$$	N

143 Sam Dale State Fish and Wildlife Area

Location: 25 miles northeast of Mount Vernon
Season: Year-round
Sites: 70 sites with electrical hookups, 18 tenting sites
Maximum length: 40 feet
Facilities: Tables, grills, vault toilets, water, dump station, boat launch, playground, concessions, restaurant, beach
Fee per night: $-$$
Management: Illinois Department of Natural Resources
Contact: (618) 835-2292; http://dnr.state.il.us/lands/landmgt/parks/r5/samdale.htm; reservations accepted
Finding the campground: From I-57 north of Mount Vernon, take exit 109 east. Follow IL 161 nearly to Johnsonville. The park entrance is on the left. Coming from US 45 to the east, head west on CR 16 in Cisne. Continue heading west through Johnsonville on IL 161. The park entrance is on the right.
UTM coordinates: 16S, 361293 E, 4267040 N
About the campground: The sign on the side of the concession building at this park telling visitors that they've reached the "middle of nowhere" is not too far off the mark. This quiet, densely wooded park is located far off the beaten path. Two conventional camping areas and one walk-in tenting area sit on the shore of the picturesque 194-acre lake. Camping areas provide a mix of flat and gently rolling terrain; oak, maple, hickory, and tulip trees provide campers with plenty of

shade. The hiking trail in the north section of the park takes you through groves of stately oaks and stands of fragrant pine. As the trail brushes against the wooded shores of Sam Dale Lake, you'll likely see great blue herons fishing near the banks.

144 Sam Parr State Park

Location: 23 miles southeast of Effingham
Season: Year-round
Sites: 32 sites with electrical and water hookups, 35 tent camping sites
Maximum length: 45 feet
Facilities: Tables, fire rings, grills, vault toilets, water, dump station, playground, picnic shelters, boat launch
Fee per night: $–$$
Management: Illinois Department of Natural Resources
Contact: (618) 783-2661; http://dnr.state.il.us/lands/landmgt/parks/r5/samparr.htm
Finding the campground: From I-70 near Greenup, follow IL 130 south. Turn left on IL 33. The park entrance is on the left. From Olney to the south, follow IL 130 north to IL 33 and turn right.
UTM coordinates: 16S, 402528 E, 4318958 N

The campsites at Sam Parr State Park are situated beside a lake.

About the campground: Thick groves of maple trees provide ample shade for the sites at Sam Parr State Park. Tent campers may stake their claim on a rolling grassy patch of land at the edge of the lake. Some of the sites in the RV campground extend out on fingers of land into the lake. Keep watch for wild turkeys; flickers and bluebirds dart among the maples and redbud trees in the campgrounds. Visitors will enjoy patches of restored prairie in the park, as well as 2 miles of foot trails and 13 miles of equestrian trails. A few miles east of the park on IL 33, watch first-run films in the middle of a cornfield (literally) at the Fairview Drive-In.

145 Oblong Park and Lake

Location: About 35 miles east of Effingham
Season: Year-round
Sites: 10 sites with electrical hookups
Maximum length: 45 feet
Facilities: Tables, fire rings, flush toilets, showers, water, dump station, short walking trail
Fee per night: $$
Management: Village of Oblong
Contact: (618) 592-3431; www.villageofoblong.com/camping.html
Finding the campground: From I-70 near Greenup, follow IL 130 south. Turn left on IL 33. In Oblong, look for signs to Oblong Park and Lake on the east side of the village. From Olney to the south, follow IL 130 north to IL 33. Turn right and follow IL 33 into Oblong.
UTM coordinates: 16S, 422162 E, 4317438 N
About the campground: This village-owned campground sits in a shaded, grassy clearing at the edge of the Crawford County Fairgrounds. A collection of antique tractor engines, the village water tower, and the fair's exhibit buildings are all a stone's throw from the camping area. Also nearby is a pleasant little lake, which contains a spurting fountain and a shoreside trail. On the west side of Oblong, the Illinois Oilfield Museum features exhibits about local oil drilling. The county fair opens in late July, and an antique tractor engine show sets up shop the second week of Aug.

146 Leaverton Park

Location: 52 miles east of Effingham
Season: Mid-Apr to mid-Nov
Sites: 400 sites with electrical and water hookups, 100 sites with no hookups
Maximum length: 45 feet
Facilities: Tables, fire rings, flush toilets, showers, water, dump station, ball fields, playground
Fee per night: $$
Management: Village of Palestine
Contact: (618) 586-2222; (618) 586-2147 for reservations
Finding the campground: From I-70 near Greenup, follow IL 130 south. Turn left on IL 33. In Palestine, turn left on Lammotte Street. Turn right on North 1875th Street. The entrance to the park and campground is on the left.

UTM coordinates: 16S, 448221 E, 4316128 N

About the campground: This campground, partly fringed by bottomland woods, is located at a municipal park with ball fields and a rodeo arena. The landscape of the campground is flat, grassy, and mostly shaded by oak trees; sites are snugly situated. Less than a mile from the campground and park, the village of Palestine features a historic opera house and bank building, as well as antique stores and a bookstore. The campground gets a workout each Labor Day weekend when the Palestine Rodeo opens its gates.

147 Ouabache Trails Park

Location: In Indiana, 5 miles north of Vincennes, Indiana
Season: Beginning of Mar to end of Nov
Sites: 35 sites with hookups for electricity and water, 9 tenting sites
Maximum length: 40 feet
Facilities: Tables, grills, flush toilets, showers, water, dump station, picnic shelter, playgrounds, laundry facility, hiking trails, cabins
Fee per night: $$
Management: Knox County Parks and Recreation
Contact: (812) 882-4316; www.knoxcountyparks.com
Finding the campground: From I-57 north of Mount Vernon, head east on US 50. After entering Indiana, exit US 50 south on IN 61. Turn right on Old State Road 67. Turn right on Second Street and immediately turn left on State Road 61. Turn Left on Old Terre Haute Road and then turn right on Fort Knox Drive, which takes you into the park.
UTM coordinates: 16S, 456033 E, 4286352 N
About the campground: As you enter Ouabache Trails Park, great views of the Ohio River and its wooded banks open up in front of you. The campground is perched on a bluff, laden with maple trees, above the river. Some campsites are tucked away in small nooks created by the rugged terrain. The park is laced with small streams and wooded ravines that lead down to the flat floodplain, where you'll find ball fields and picnicking facilities. While the park itself is fairly new, the land it occupies possesses a rich history. Many Native American relics have been found in the park, and an outdoor exhibit commemorating a former English fort is located on a high bluff near the park's entrance.

148 Kimmell Park

Location: The northern edge of Vincennes, Indiana
Season: Beginning of Apr to end of Oct
Sites: 10 sites with no hookups, 15 tent camping sites
Maximum length: 40 feet
Facilities: Tables, fire rings, flush toilets, showers, water, boat ramp, picnic pavilion, playground, basketball court
Fee per night: $-$$

Management: City of Vincennes

Contact: (812) 882-1140; www.vincennesparks.com/parks

Finding the campground: From I-57 north of Mount Vernon, head east on US 50 into Indiana. Exit at IN 61 and head south. Turn right on East St. Clair Street. Curve to the right on Oliphant Drive and enter the park on the left.

UTM coordinates: 16S, 454992 E, 4283299 N

About the campground: This municipal campground, located on the outskirts of Vincennes, Indiana, sits on the shore of the Ohio River. Little shade is available in the grassy camping area. The adjoining bottomland woods host a collection of hiking trails. Attractive stone platforms within the park offer ideal picnicking spots. A steel trestle bridge spans the river south of the park. Despite the earthen levee that separates the campground from the one-hundred-year-old steel mill across the road, some sounds from the mill may drift into the campground. Vincennes, the oldest city in Indiana, hosts a number of attractions, including several small museums and the George Rogers Clark National Historic Park.

149 Red Hills State Park

Location: 14 miles east of Olney

Season: Year-round

Sites: 100 sites with electrical hookups, 20 walk-in sites

Maximum length: 40 feet

Facilities: Tables, grills, flush toilets, showers, water, dump station, hiking and equestrian trails, picnicking shelters, park restaurant

Fee per night: $-$$$

Management: Illinois Department of Natural Resources

Contact: (618) 936-2469; http://dnr.state.il.us/lands/landmgt/parks/r5/redhls.htm

Finding the campground: From I-57/I-70 in Effingham, head southeast on IL 33. In Newton, turn right on IL 130 and follow it to US 50. Turn left on US 50. The entrance to the park's camping areas is on the right.

UTM coordinates: 16S, 427515 E, 4286453 N

About the campground: All campsites at this medium-sized state park are well shaded with maple, oak, and beech trees. A handful of sites at the main campground are nestled against a forty-acre lake. The nearby tenting campground, which occupies a gently sloping bank on the shore of the lake, is active with birds flitting among the trees. The park's restaurant offers a dining area overlooking the lake. A 2-mile hiking trail in the northern section of the park runs through wooded ravines that in spring and summer are sprinkled with wildflowers. Continuing to the top of Red Hill, the trail provides commanding views of the surrounding pastoral landscape. The park sits on the boundary that once was the westernmost edge of the first land in Illinois ceded by Native Americans to the United States.

The trail at Red Hills State Park runs through wooded ravines on its way to an overlook.

150 Beall Woods State Park

Location: About 60 miles east of Mount Vernon
Season: Year-round
Sites: 16 sites with no hookups
Maximum length: 30 feet
Facilities: Tables, grills, vault toilets, water, fishing dock, hiking trails
Fee per night: $
Management: Illinois Department of Natural Resources
Contact: (618) 298-2442; http://dnr.state.il.us/lands/landmgt/parks/r5/beall.htm
Finding the campground: On I-64 just west of the Indiana state line, head north on IL 1. In Keensburg, turn right on First Street, and left on North 900 Boulevard. The park entrance is on the left.
UTM coordinates: 16S, 427036 E, 4244921 N

A small fishing lake is a stone's throw away from the campground at Beall Woods State Park.

About the campground: This small, shaded campground sits in a large grassy area on a rise overlooking the fishing docks and picnic area of a small fifteen-acre lake. Sites are generously sized, but offer no privacy. The main attraction at Beall Woods are the trails along Coffee Creek and the Ohio River, where you'll encounter over sixty different species of elms, hickories, beeches, maples, and other types of trees. Ask in the visitor center for the location of the sycamore tree with a trunk 18 feet in circumference. The visitor center offers an impressive display of exhibits about the natural history of the park and local naturalists who performed research there. Check in with staff before hiking: Some parts of the park are prone to flooding.

151 Hilltop

Location: About 60 miles east of Mount Vernon
Season: Year-round
Sites: 20 sites with electrical and water hookups
Maximum length: 40 feet
Facilities: Tables, grills, flush toilets, showers, water, dump station, picnicking area, swimming pool, boat ramp
Fee per night: $$
Management: City of Grayville
Contact: (618) 375-3671
Finding the campground: From IL 1 in Grayville, head east on East North Street. Turn right on South Water Street and turn left on Lake Street. Coming from I-64 to the south, exit on IL 1 (South Court Street) and turn left (north). Turn right on CR 2450 North. Turn left on CR 2125 East (South Water Street) and turn right on Lake Street.
UTM coordinates: 16S, 413717 E, 4233592 N
About the campground: This appropriately named campground rests on the flat top of a wooded bluff 100 feet above the Wabash River. The spacious, well-shaded sites are surrounded by steep ravines. Down the bluff from the campground is a municipal park with ball diamonds, tennis courts, a swimming pool, a sand volleyball court, and a great overlook of the Wabash River Valley. The park is located at the southedge of Grayville, a pleasant little town located on a hairpin turn in the Wabash River. Ask in city hall for a brochure that describes a walking tour of the historical markers within the town.

152 Harmonie State Park

Location: In Indiana, 20 miles northwest of Evansville, Indiana
Season: Beginning Apr to end of Nov
Sites: 200 sites with electrical hookups; wheelchair-sites available
Maximum length: 40 feet
Facilities: Tables, grills, flush toilets, showers, water, dump station, cabins, nature center, hiking, equestrian and bike trails, boat launch, picnic shelters, fishing ponds
Fee per night: $$–$$$

Management: Indiana Department of Natural Resources
Contact: (812) 682-4821; www.in.gov/dnr/parklake/2981.htm; (866) 622-6746 for reservations
Finding the campground: Head east on I-64 into Indiana. Turn south on IN 69. After passing the turn for New Harmony, turn right on IN 269 and enter the park. From the south, take IL 141/IN 62 east to IN 69 in Mount Vernon. Turn left on IN 69, and turn left again on IN 269 to enter the park.
UTM coordinates: 16S, 417341 E, 4213562 N
About the campground: This sprawling, newly constructed campground is mostly open and well shaded. Groves of sycamore and tulip trees line the campground's many cul-de-sacs. The park's terrain ranges from flat floodplain along the Wabash River to gently rolling hills of the camping area to plunging ravines along the interior trails that crisscross the park. On the park's trails, you'll encounter steep bluffs and sandy-bottom streams. Towering specimens of maple and oak, lush greenery, and hanging vines evoke the atmosphere of a primeval forest. The nearby village of New Harmony was the site of two of America's earliest utopian communities. Visitors can tour historic buildings and learn about these social movements of the early 1800s.

153 Burrell Park

Location: 45 miles southeast of Mount Vernon
Season: Mid-Apr to mid-Oct
Sites: 20 sites with hookups for water, electricity, and sewer; 25 sites with no hookups
Maximum length: 45 feet
Facilities: Tables, grills, flush toilets, showers, water, tables, playgrounds, picnic shelters, fishing pond
Fee per night: $–$$
Management: City of Carmi
Contact: (618) 382-2693; www.cityofcarmi.com/recreation.htm#
Finding the campground: From IL 1/14 in Carmi, head west on Stewart Street. Follow Stewart Street as it turns right and becomes CR 1000 East. The entrance to the park is on the left.
UTM coordinates: 16S, 395395 E, 4217372 N
About the campground: Enter the park through a brick gateway, and you'll find a small, mostly shaded campground. Little wooded bluffs accompany a small creek that runs through this well-maintained park. The park also hosts a tiny fishing pond and a short walking trail. Orlando Burrell—a local figure who served as a civil war officer, mayor, judge, sheriff, and U.S. congressman—donated land for the park. In downtown Carmi, across from the courthouse, is a castlelike brick and limestone building from the late 1800s featuring three turreted towers.

154 Hamilton County State Fish and Wildlife Area

Location: 40 miles southeast of Mount Vernon
Season: Year-round
Sites: 60 sites with electrical hookups
Maximum Length: 40 feet
Facilities: Flush toilets, grills, showers, water, tables, dump station, picnic shelter, boat launch, hiking trails
Fee per night: $$
Management: Illinois Department of Natural Resources
Contact: (618) 773-4340; http://dnr.state.il.us/lands/landmgt/parks/r5/hamilton.htm
Finding the campground: From I-64 near Mount Vernon, head southeast on IL 142. In McLeansboro, go east on IL 14. Turn right on CR 125 East.
UTM coordinates: 16S, 376600 E, 4212911 N
About the campground: Some sites at this campground are a dozen feet from the shore of Dolan Lake, and each site has a view of the lake. The camping area is well shaded with stands of pine. The tranquil atmosphere gets busy during the height of summer. Hikers can explore the park's gently rolling hills and open fields by following a trail for 3 miles around the lake. Anglers fish the seventy-five-acre lake for largemouth bass, bluegill, sunfish, crappie, channel catfish, and bullheads.

Shawnee National Forest East Side

	Hookup Sites	Total Sites	Max RV Length	Hookups	Toilets	Showers	Drinking Water	Dump Station	Recreation	Fee	Reservations
155 Saline County Fish and Wildlife Area	0	43	40	N/A	NF	N	Y	Y	H, F, L, R	$	N
156 Garden of the Gods Recreation Area	0	12	35	N/A	NF	N	Y	N	H, R	$	N
157 Pounds Hollow Recreation Area	0	76	40	N/A	NF	Y	Y	Y	H, F, S	$	N
158 Camp Cadiz	0	11	40	N/A	NF	N	Y	N	H	$	N
159 Cave-in-Rock State Park	34	59	45	E	F	Y	Y	Y	H, F	$$-$$$	N
160 Cave-in-Rock Village	10	10	30	E	NF	N	Y	N	F	$$	N
161 Tower Rock	0	25	40	N/A	NF	N	Y	N	F, L	$	N
162 Rauchfuss Hill State Recreation Area	0	20	40	N/A	NF	N	Y	Y	H	$	N

155 Saline County Fish and Wildlife Area

Location: 15 miles southeast of Harrisburg
Season: Year-round
Sites: 43 sites with no hookups
Maximum length: 40 feet
Facilities: Tables, grills, vault toilets, water, tables, dump station, playground, picnic shelter, boat launches, fishing docks, equestrian camping area, hiking and equestrian trails
Fee per night: $
Management: Illinois Department of Natural Resources
Contact: (618) 276-4405; http://dnr.state.il.us/Lands/Landmgt/parks/r5/saline.htm
Finding the campground: From Harrisburg, head east on IL 13. Turn right on IL 142. Turn right on Shawnee Forest Road (CR 7). The park entrance is on the right.
UTM coordinates: 16S, 378306 E, 4172382 N
About the campground: A small attractive lake cradled by the northernmost Shawnee Hills serves as the centerpiece of Saline County Fish and Wildlife Area. Sweet gum and tulip trees provide plenty of shade for the campsites. Half of the sites sit on the sloping banks of Glen O. Jones Lake, and the other half are perched on the high wooded bluff above the lake. Also up on the bluff is a bronze statue of Tecumseh, a Shawnee chief who attempted to unite Native American tribes to prevent the encroachment from white settlers. Native Americans and European settlers harvested salt from the salt springs that once existed in the park.

The lake at Saline County Fish and Wildlife Area is cradled by wooded hills of the Shawnee National Forest.

156 Garden of the Gods Recreation Area

Location: 20 miles southeast of Harrisburg
Season: Year-round
Sites: 12 sites with no hookups
Maximum length: 35 feet
Facilities: Tables, grills, vault toilets, water, hiking and equestrian trails
Fee per night: $
Management: Shawnee National Forest
Contact: (618) 658-2111; www.fs.fed.us/r9/forests/shawnee/recreation/camping/pharaoh/
Finding the campground: From Harrisburg, head south on IL 145. Turn left on IL 34, and then turn left on Karbers Ridge Road (CR 4). Turn left again on Garden of the Gods Road. The entrance is on the left. Follow signs to Pharaoh Campground.
UTM coordinates: 16S, 378213 E, 4162371 N
About the campground: It's for good reason that Garden of the Gods is such a popular destination in southern Illinois. At the edge of the main parking area, visitors can stand atop strangely shaped rock formations and take in 30-mile views of distant rolling hills. The campground, a short walk from the rock formations, is a gently rolling area on the top of a ridge. A canopy of

Garden of the Gods features dramatic rock formations and great hiking trails.

pine boughs offers shade for the well-spaced campsites. Excellent hiking trails wind throughout the area. Be sure to check out the trail that runs next to the sandstone cliffs and small canyons between the campground and the park road. If rain has fallen recently, you'll encounter a picturesque waterfall along this trail.

157 Pounds Hollow Recreation Area

Location: 15 miles north of Cave-in-Rock
Season: Beginning of Apr to mid-Dec
Sites: 76 sites with no hookups
Maximum length: 40 feet
Facilities: Tables, grills, vault toilets, water, picnic area, dump station, hiking trails, beach, showers (at Pounds Hollow Lake)
Fee per night: $
Management: Shawnee National Forest
Contact: (618) 658-2111; www.fs.fed.us/r9/forests/shawnee/recreation/camping/pineridge/
Finding the campground: From Harrisburg, head east on Highway 13. Turn right on Highway 1, and then turn right on Pounds Hollow Road. The entrance to Pounds Hollow Recreation Area is on the right. Follow signs for the Pine Ridge Campground.
UTM coordinates: 16S, 388136 E, 4163652 N
About the campground: Ravines sprinkled with dogwood trees border many of the campsites. The flat camping area, well shaded with maple trees, sits on a steep bluff above a small lake. Pounds Hollow Lake is nestled in a deep wooded valley. On muggy summer days, the lake's beach brings in people from miles around. Nearby, you'll find plenty of trails to hike at Rim Rock and Garden of the Gods.

158 Camp Cadiz

Location: 10 miles north of Cave-in-Rock
Season: Beginning of Apr to mid-Dec
Sites: 11 sites with no hookups
Maximum length: 40 feet
Facilities: Vault toilets, fire rings, water, picnic tables
Fee per night: $
Management: Shawnee National Forest
Contact: (618) 658-2111; www.fs.fed.us/r9/forests/shawnee/recreation/camping/cadiz/
Finding the campground: From Harrisburg, head south on IL 145. Turn left on IL 34, and then turn left on Karbers Ridge Road. Turn right on Cadiz Road. The campground will be the left.
UTM coordinates: 16S, 390113 E, 4159563 N
About the campground: Visitors to Camp Cadiz will enjoy the fragrance of pine trees and a very quiet atmosphere at this out-of-the-way spot. The campground is well shaded, flat, and surrounded by beautiful roads winding through the forest. Remnants of a depression-era Civilian Conservation Corps camp are visible within the campground. Many come to this basic campground for

hiking because it serves as one of the trailheads for the 146-mile River to River Trail, as well the Beaver Trail, which leads to a nearby formation called Rim Rock.

159 Cave-in-Rock State Park

Location: Less than 1 mile east of the town of Cave-in-Rock on the shore of the Ohio River
Season: Year-round
Sites: 34 sites with electrical hookups, 25 sites with no hookups, several wheelchair-accessible sites
Maximum length: 45 feet
Facilities: Tables, grills, flush toilets, showers, water, picnic area, dump station, playgrounds, restaurant, cabins
Fee per night: $$–$$$
Management: Illinois Department of Natural Resources
Contact: (618) 289-4325; http://dnr.state.il.us/lands/Landmgt/parks/r5/caverock.htm
Finding the campground: From Harrisburg, head east on IL 13. Turn right on IL 1. In the town of Cave-in-Rock, turn left on Main Street and follow signs to the state park.
UTM coordinates: 16S, 397623 E, 4147514 N
About the campground: This well-maintained campground is spread out within a sprawling grassy area laden with shade trees. A separate tent camping area is secluded and nicely wooded, but most of the sites have gently sloping surfaces. The park offers many places to watch riverboat traffic on the Ohio River, including an indoor/outdoor restaurant and cabins on the bluff. Also on the bluff is a series of outstanding picnicking spots. The deep sandstone cave for which the park is named claims a rich history: It once hosted a tavern, it served as a set for the film *How the West Was Won,* and at various times served as a hideout for bandits and river pirates.

160 Cave-in-Rock Village

Location: Next to the ferry landing in downtown Cave-in-Rock on the shore of the Ohio River
Season: Year-round
Sites: 10 sites with electrical hookups
Maximum length: 30 feet
Facilities: Tables, vault toilets, water, picnic area, playground
Fee per night: $$
Management: Village of Cave-in-Rock
Contact: (618) 289-3238
Finding the campground: From Harrisburg, head east on IL 13. Turn right on IL 1. The campground is located to the left of the ferry landing.
UTM coordinates: 16S, 396924 E, 4147121 N
About the campground: This diminutive municipal campground occupies a flat grassy bottomland between the Ohio River and the village of Cave-in-Rock's tiny downtown. The campground is open and fairly shaded, and is located next to the free car ferry that takes passengers across the Ohio River. 0.5-mile to the east is the entrance to Cave-in-Rock State Park.

Cave-in-Rock, located on the shore of the Ohio River, once served as a hideout for river pirates.

161 Tower Rock

Location: 5 miles east of Elizabethtown on the shore of the Ohio River
Season: Beginning of May to mid-Dec
Sites: 25 sites with no hookups
Maximum length: 40 feet
Facilities: Tables, grills, vault toilets, water, picnic area, boat launch
Fee per night: $
Management: Shawnee National Forest
Contact: (618) 658-2111; www.fs.fed.us/r9/forests/shawnee/recreation/camping/towerrock/
Finding the campground: From Harrisburg, take IL 145 south. Turn left on IL 34. Turn left on IL 146 and pass through Elizabethtown. Turn right on Tower Rock Road and follow signs to the campground.
UTM coordinates: 16S, 391189 E, 4146267 N
About the campground: This campground is situated within dense bottomland forest. The campsites are spacious and open with no natural buffers between them. Bluffs and steep ravines border the camping area's north side, while the south side faces the sandy shore of the Ohio River. The river is more than 0.5 mile wide here and flows around a couple of wooded islands. After the annual flooding subsides, debris within the campground must be cleaned up. Be sure to call ahead, especially if visiting early in the season.

162 Rauchfuss Hill State Recreation Area

Location: 1 mile north of Golconda near the Ohio River
Season: Beginning of May to end of Oct
Sites: 20 sites with no hookups
Maximum length: 40 feet
Facilities: Vault toilets, grills, water, picnic area, hiking trails, dump station
Fee per night: $
Management: Illinois Department of Natural Resources
Contact: (618) 949-3304
Finding the campground: From Harrisburg, take IL 145 south. Turn left on IL 34. Turn left on IL 146. Before reaching Golconda, look for the entrance to the camping area on the left.
UTM coordinates: 16S, 368669 E, 4137441 N
About the campground: Perched on a bluff 250 feet above the Ohio River, this small campground offers groves of pine trees, hiking trails, and fine views of the river. Because it offers such a good vantage point for watching riverboat traffic, the bluff also has been known as Steamboat Hill. Nestled against the bottom of the bluff is the Golconda Marina, a 200-slip, state-owned facility that is connected to the campground with a walking trail. The marina provides access to prime fishing grounds created with a lock and dam near Smithland, Kentucky. Beyond the marina is the pleasant village of Golconda, containing a restaurant and a few shops.

Shawnee National Forest West Side

	Hookup Sites	Total Sites	Max RV Length	Hookups	Toilets	Showers	Drinking Water	Dump Station	Recreation	Fee	Reservations
163 Bell Smith Springs Recreation Area	0	21	40	N/A	NF	N	Y	N	H	$	N
164 Lake Glendale Recreation Area	31	57	40	E	F	Y	Y	Y	H, F, L, S	$$	N
165 Dixon Springs State Park	39	49	40	E	NF	Y	Y	Y	H, S	$-$$$	N
166 Ferne Clyffe State Park	59	71	50	E	F	Y	Y	Y	H, F, R, S	$-$$$	N
167 Giant City State Park	85	99	38	E	F	Y	Y	Y	H, F, L, R, S	$-$$$	N
168 Devils Kitchen Lake	0	8	N/A	N/A	F	Y	Y	N	F, L	$$	N
169 Little Grassy Lake	75	145	40	E, S, W	F	Y	Y	Y	F, L	$$	N
170 Crab Orchard Lake	122	250	45	E	F	Y	Y	Y	F, B, L	$$	N
171 Lake Murphysboro State Park	54	74	45	E	F	Y	Y	Y	H, F, L	$$-$$$	N
172 Kincaid Lake Marina	28	36	50	E, S, W	NF	Y	Y	Y	B, F, L, S	$$-$$$	N
173 Johnson Creek Recreation Area	0	20	40	N/A	NF	N	Y	Y	H, F, L, R, S	$	N
174 Turkey Bayou	0	5	35	N/A	N	N	N	N	F, L	Free	N
175 Devil's Backbone Park	51	51	45	E, W	F	Y	Y	Y	H, F	$$	N
176 Trail of Tears State Forest	0	14	20	N/A	NF	N	Y	N	H	$	Y
177 Pine Hills	0	13	35	N/A	NF	N	Y	N	H	$	N
178 Thebes	25	25	40	E, S, W	N	N	N	N	F, L	$$	Y
179 Horseshoe Lake State Fish and Wildlife Area	78	88	40	E	F	Y	Y	Y	H, F, L, B	$$-$$$	N
180 Grand Chain	25	35	45	E, S, W	F	Y	Y	Y	F	$$	Y
181 Fort Massac State Park	50	57	40	E	F	Y	Y	Y	H, F, L	$$-$$$	N

163 Bell Smith Springs Recreation Area

Location: 18 miles south of Harrisburg
Season: Year-round
Sites: 21 sites with no hookups
Maximum length: 40 feet
Facilities: Vault toilets, water, grills, picnic tables, hiking trails
Fee per night: $
Management: Shawnee National Forest
Contact: (618) 658-2111; www.fs.fed.us/r9/forests/shawnee/recreation/camping/redbud/
Finding the campground: Heading south on IL 145 from Harrisburg, turn right on Water Tower Road. Turn right on Ozark Road (CR 3100 North), and then turn left on Bell Smith Springs Road (CR 350 East) and follow signs for the Redbud Campground.
UTM coordinates: 16S, 353618 E, 4154025 N
About the campground: The fairly private campsites possess ample buffer zones between them, and are well shaded by mature specimens of oak and maple. This gloriously remote campground is situated next to a series of dramatic sandstone canyons. The trails that tour the canyon are some of the best in the state. The combination of natural springs and the convergence of four creeks ensure rich displays of wildflowers for much of the year. The creek's clear water often takes on a sapphire hue. A favorite spot is the 30-foot-high natural arch.

164 Lake Glendale Recreation Area

Location: 10 miles east of Vienna
Season: Year-round
Sites: 31 sites with electrical hookups, 26 sites with no hookups
Maximum length: 40 feet
Facilities: Flush toilets, showers, grills, water, picnic area, dump station, beach, boat launch (electric motors only), hiking trails
Fee per night: $$
Management: Private concessioners/Shawnee National Forest
Contact: (618) 949-3807; www.lakeglendale.net/
Finding the campground: From I-24 near Vienna, head east on IL 146. Turn left on IL 145. The entrance to the park is a couple of miles ahead on the right. Follow signs for the Oak Point Campground.
UTM coordinates: 16S, 352965 E, 4141429 N
About the campground: The spacious campsites at Lake Glendale are nicely spread out under a canopy of maple, oak, and pine trees. The camping area is mostly flat; some sites offer views of the eighty-acre lake. Across the lake from the campground is a large picnic area and beach. A long hiking trail loops around the lake. Lake Glendale offers easy access to various destinations in the area, such as Bell Smith Springs Recreation Area, the Tunnel Hill Trail, and the Cache River Natural Area.

165 Dixon Springs State Park

Location: 9 miles west of Vienna
Season: Year-round
Sites: 39 sites with electrical hookups, 10 walk-in sites
Maximum length: 40 feet
Facilities: Vault toilets, grills, showers (at pool), water, picnic shelters, dump station, outdoor pool with 40-foot waterslide, hiking trails
Fee per night: $–$$$
Management: Illinois Department of Natural Resources
Contact: (618) 949-3394; http://dnr.state.il.us/Lands/Landmgt/parks/r5/dixon.htm
Finding the campground: From I-24 near Vienna, head east on IL 146. The entrance to the park is on the left after passing IL 145.
UTM coordinates: 16S, 352407 E, 4138581 N
About the campground: The campgrounds at Dixon Springs are well maintained and inviting, particularly the spacious walk-in sites, which sit within a grove of 70-foot-tall pine trees. The main campground is well shaded and compact; some sites toward the back offer more privacy. The park's rocky outcroppings and natural springs have attracted many generations of local visitors. Beginning in the 1850s, a resort operated at the park, and prior to that, stories suggest that Native Americans used the park for similar purposes. The small wooden churches on the hill within the park are remnants of a former small town. The locally renowned chocolate shop near the park's entrance may require a moment of your time.

166 Ferne Clyffe State Park

Location: 30 miles southeast of Carbondale
Season: Year-round
Sites: 59 sites with electrical hookups, 12 walk-in sites; wheelchair-accessible sites available
Maximum length: 50 feet
Facilities: Tables, grills, flush toilets, showers, water, dump station, horse campground, fishing pond, hiking trails
Fee per night: $–$$$
Management: Illinois Department of Natural Resources
Contact: (618) 995-2411; http://dnr.state.il.us/lands/Landmgt/parks/r5/ferne.htm
Finding the campground: From Carbondale, take IL 13 east. Head south on I-57. Follow I-24 as it splits toward the southeast. Exit west on Tunnel Hill road (CR 12). Turn left on IL 37 and immediately look for the park entrance on the right.
UTM coordinates: 16S, 325241 E, 4156347 N
About the campground: This out-of-the-way park is loaded with pristine hiking trails that take you to sandstone cliffs and over big wooded bluffs. The main camping area is flat with gravel pads; the area is fairly open with stands of maple and oak offering shade. The walk-in sites, tucked away south of the main campground, afford plenty of wooded privacy; some sites are

located on the edge of a bluff. Cast a line in the sixteen-acre lake for largemouth bass, bluegill, and channel catfish (boats not allowed). Don't miss the 100-foot intermittent waterfall on the Big Rocky Hollow Trail.

167 Giant City State Park

Location: 11 miles south of Carbondale
Season: Year-round
Sites: 85 sites with electrical hookups, 14 walk-in sites
Maximum length: 38 feet
Facilities: Flush toilets, grills, showers, water, tables, dump station, boat launch, hiking trails, visitor center, lodge, restaurant, picnic shelters
Fee per night: $-$$$
Management: Illinois Department of Natural Resources
Contact: (618) 457-4836; http://dnr.state.il.us/lands/landmgt/parks/r5/gc.htm
Finding the campground: From Carbondale, head south on US 51. Turn left on Makanda Road and follow signs into the park.
UTM coordinates: 16S, 308580 E, 4163855 N
About the campground: This sprawling campground resides within one of the premier state parks in Illinois. The gently rolling terrain is heavily canopied by maple and oak trees, and surrounded by dense forest. The tenting area is open, grassy, and large. The park abounds with excellent hiking trails where you'll encounter big boulders, sandstone cliffs, small waterfalls, and a variety of wildflowers and ferns. Ivy clings to the rocky cliffs and hardwoods tower overhead in the dense upland forests. Campers may be serenaded in the morning by the park's thriving population of wild turkeys. They gobble all year long, but reach their zenith in Apr as hens prepare for egg laying.

168 Devils Kitchen Lake

Location: About 15 miles southeast of Carbondale
Season: Beginning of Apr to the end of Oct
Sites: 8 walk-in sites
Maximum length: N/A
Facilities: Tables, grills, flush toilets, showers, water, boat launch
Fee per night: $$
Management: U.S. Fish and Wildlife Service
Contact: (618) 457-5004
Finding the campground: In Carbondale, head east on IL 13. Turn right on North Giant City Road (CR 12). Turn left on Grassy Road, and then turn right on Rocky Comfort Road. Turn left on CR 215 North (West Devil's Kitchen Road).
UTM coordinates: 16S, 315111 E, 4165346 N
About the campground: The open and grassy camping area sits on a knoll about 100 feet from the wooded shore of Devils Kitchen Lake. The sites, anywhere from 50 to 200 feet from the parking area,

have ample space between them. Anglers fish for bass and rainbow trout in the 810-acre lake. Hills continuously rise up from the shoreline of this multi-armed lake.

169 Little Grassy Lake

Location: 10 miles south of Carbondale
Season: Beginning of Apr to end of Oct
Sites: 60 sites with electrical and water hookups; 15 sites with electrical, water, and sewer hookups; 70 sites with no hookups
Maximum length: 40 feet
Facilities: Tables, grills, flush toilets, showers, water, dump station, boat launch, marina, camp store, playground
Fee per night: $$
Management: Owned by the U.S. Fish and Wildlife Service and privately managed
Contact: (618) 457-6655
Finding the campground: In Carbondale, head east on IL 13. Turn right on North Giant City Road (CR 12). Turn left on Grassy Road, and then turn right on Hidden Bay Lane.
UTM coordinates: 16S, 310267 E, 4168244 N
About the campground: Set on a small bluff above Grassy Lake, this campground is active with anglers and boaters taking advantage of the attractive 1,200-acre lake. Campsites occupy a couple of wooded peninsulas; the terrain is flat or gently sloping. The curving shoreline of Grassy Lake provides an attractive backdrop for many of the campsites. The area near the small marina is often dense with RVs, whereas tent camping sites closer to the entrance are much quieter. At the state-operated fish hatchery down the road, visitors can observe fish-breeding procedures through glass windows and step out on a platform overlooking the outdoor holding tanks.

170 Crab Orchard Lake

Location: 6 miles east of Carbondale
Season: Beginning of Apr to end of Oct
Sites: 122 sites with electrical hookups, 128 sites with no hookups
Maximum length: 45 feet
Facilities: Tables, grills, flush toilets, showers, water, dump station, picnicking area, boat launch, beach
Fee per night: $$
Management: Owned by the U.S. Fish and Wildlife Service and privately managed
Contact: (618) 985-4983
Finding the campground: In Carbondale, head east on IL 13. After passing US 51, turn right on Campground Drive.
UTM coordinates: 16S, 313386 E, 4178912 N
About the campground: For campers who prefer a busy atmosphere, this large, open campground will be the place to go. The sites occupy a flat wooded peninsula that reaches out

into the tree-fringed lake. Boaters, jet skiers, and anglers flock to Crab Orchard Lake, the largest lake among the three human-made lakes within the Crab Orchard National Wildlife Refuge. Crab Orchard Lake was created in 1938 and occupies about 7,000 acres. Nearby, a variety of restaurants and stores line IL 13 on the way into Carbondale.

171 Lake Murphysboro State Park

Location: 10 miles west of Carbondale
Season: Year-round
Sites: 54 sites with electrical hookups, 20 sites with no hookups
Maximum length: 45 feet
Facilities: Tables, grills, flush toilets, showers (at boat docks), water, dump station, boat launch, hiking trail, playground
Fee per night: $$–$$$
Management: Illinois Department of Natural Resources
Contact: (618) 684-2867; http://dnr.state.il.us/lands/Landmgt/parks/r5/murphysb.htm
Finding the campground: From Carbondale, head west on IL 13. In Murphysboro, continue straight ahead (west) on IL 149. The entrance to the park is on the right.
UTM coordinates: 16S, 290115 E, 4183840 N
About the campground: The terrain around Lake Murphysboro is rugged and thick with oak and hickory. The main campground—which sits on a finger of land stretching into the lake—is flat and compact. You can watch the fish jump from the well-spaced and well-shaded tent camping sites nestled at the edge of the water. The 600-foot-long earthen dam at the south end of the park affords good views of this picturesque 145-acre lake. Murphysboro, located 2 miles east, contains a variety of restaurants and stores.

172 Kincaid Lake Marina

Location: 12 miles northwest of Carbondale
Season: Beginning of May to end of Oct
Sites: 28 sites with water, electrical, and sewer hookups; 8 walk-in sites
Maximum length: 50 feet
Facilities: Tables, grills, portable toilets, showers, water, dump station, full-service marina with boat rentals, cabins, bar/restaurant, guide services, groceries, boating and fishing supplies, pool
Fee per night: $$–$$$
Management: Owned by Jackson County and privately managed
Contact: (618) 687-4914
Finding the campground: From Carbondale, head west on IL 13. In Murphysboro, continue straight ahead (west) on IL 149. Turn right on Marina Road and follow it straight into the marina.
UTM coordinates: 16S, 288111 E, 4186177 N
About the campground: The main campground, located adjacent to an RV park, is small, well shaded, and partially surrounded by woodland. The nearby walk-in sites are lakeside, offer

beautiful views, and remove campers from the hubbub at the marina and the RV park. Maple and hickory trees provide shade along the rolling shoreline. Kinkaid Village Marina pulls in the anglers and the pleasure-boating crowd. Nearby is Lake Murphysboro State Park.

173 Johnson Creek Recreation Area

Location: About 20 miles northwest of Carbondale
Season: Year-round
Sites: 20 sites with no hookups
Maximum length: 40 feet
Facilities: Tables, grills, vault toilets, water, dump station, boat launch, hiking trails, beach, equestrian camping, fishing pier, beach house
Fee per night: $
Management: Shawnee National Forest
Contact: (618) 833-8576; www.fs.fed.us/r9/forests/shawnee/recreation/camping/johnson
Finding the campground: From Murphysboro, head west on IL 13. In Murphysboro, continue straight ahead (west) on IL 149. Turn right on IL 3. Turn right on IL 151. The campground is on the right. From St. Louis, take IL 3 south. Nearly 20 miles after Chester, turn left on IL 151.
UTM coordinates: 16S, 278136 E, 4190245 N
About the campground: The flat and lightly wooded campground is surrounded by rugged terrain offering excellent hiking and equestrian trails. The hiking trail follows the shore of Kinkaid Lake, where you'll find dense woodland and frequent rock formations. Kinkaid Lake, a premier fishing destination and one of the largest lakes in southern Illinois, features rock walls and many dozens of wooded inlets.

174 Turkey Bayou

Location: About 25 miles southwest of Carbondale near the shore of the Big Muddy River
Season: Year-round
Sites: 5 sites with no hookups
Maximum length: 35 feet
Facilities: Fire rings, boat launch, no drinking water available
Fee per night: Free
Management: Shawnee National Forest
Contact: (618) 833-8576; www.fs.fed.us/r9/forests/shawnee/recreation/camping/turkey/
Finding the campground: From Murphysboro, head west on IL 149. At IL 3, turn left. Turn left on Oakwood Bottom Road and follow into the camping area.
UTM coordinates: 16S, 287170 E, 4173164 N
About the campground: Turkey Bayou gets the prize for being one of Illinois' most out-of-the-way rustic campgrounds. This absolutely no-frills camping area sits between a small lake and the Big Muddy River. As the name suggests, the terrain is flat and wet. Look for the beaver lodges and birds such as white egrets and great blue herons. To the east, bluffs containing the Little Grand Canyon rise up on the other side of the Big Muddy River.

175 Devil's Backbone Park

Location: 25 miles southwest of Carbondale
Season: Beginning of May to end of Oct
Sites: 51 sites with water and electrical hookups, 7 tent camping sites
Maximum length: 45 feet
Facilities: Tables, grills, picnic shelters, flush toilets, showers, water, dump station
Fee per night: $$
Management: Village of Grand Tower
Contact: (618) 684-6192
Finding the campground: From Murphysboro, head west on IL 149. At IL 3, turn left. Turn right on Powerplant Road, and then turn left on Third Street Extension. Turn right on Twentieth Street and left on Brunkhorst Avenue. Coming from the south on IL 3, turn left on Grand Tower Road and follow it as it turns right to become Front Street. Turn left on Brunkhorst Avenue.

The campground at Devil's Backbone Park sits between a slender river bluff and the Mississippi River.

UTM coordinates: 16S, 278331 E, 4168452 N

About the campground: This campground is situated in a municipal park located between the shore of the Mississippi River and a narrow wooded bluff known as the Devil's Backbone. The shoreside sites offer minimal shade, while sites closer to the bluff are better sheltered. Explore the bluff on the hiking trail that starts near the park's entrance gate. The park has an old locomotive on display, as well as some of the coke ovens that were used in the local foundry. As with any campground on a river, be sure to call first to inquire about flooding (painted markings on the shower building show the levels of flooding in recent decades). Opposite the levee in the village of Grand Tower, check out the boat pilothouse replica and the collection of riverboat artifacts in the small Mississippi River Museum and Interpretive Center.

176 Trail of Tears State Forest

Location: 7 miles northwest of Jonesboro
Season: Year-round; from Dec 24 to May 15, campsites only accessible via foot
Sites: 14 sites (4 with 3-sided log shelters) with no hookups
Maximum length: 20 feet
Facilities: Tables, fire rings, vault toilets, water (in main picnic area), visitor center, picnic areas
Fee per night: $
Management: Illinois Department of Natural Resources
Contact: (618) 833-4910; http://dnr.state.il.us/lands/Landmgt/parks/r5/trltears.htm; reservations accepted
Finding the campground: From Carbondale, head south on US 51. Turn right on IL 146 and pass through Anna and Jonesboro. Turn right on IL 127. Turn left on State Forest Road (CR 13). The park visitor center is on the right.
UTM coordinates: 16S, 291402 E, 4151093 N
About the campground: The back roads through the rugged terrain at Trail of Tears State Forest offer a series of private camping options. The well-shaded sites are situated on narrow, rocky, ridgetops forested with black oaks, white oaks, and hickories. The park's many roads take you to gravelly streams within steep wooded ravines. The Civilian Conservation Corp left a big mark on the park in the 1930s by building the creek side stonework, attractive log shelters, and the park's numerous roads. The forest is named for an event in 1838 and 1839 when the Cherokee, Creek, and Chickasaw Native American tribes were forced by the U.S. military to give up their lands in the southeast U.S. and move to the Oklahoma Territory. When they overwintered 2 miles south of this forest, many lives were lost.

177 Pine Hills

Location: 5 miles northwest of Jonesboro
Season: Mid-Mar to mid-Dec
Sites: 13 sites with no hookups
Maximum length: 35 feet
Facilities: Vault toilets, grills, water, tables, hiking trails
Fee per night: $
Management: Shawnee National Forest
Contact: (618) 833-8576; www.fs.fed.us/r9/forests/shawnee/recreation/camping/pinehills/
Finding the campground: From Carbondale, head south on US 51. Turn right on IL 146 and pass through Anna and Jonesboro. Continue west on IL 146 and then turn right on IL 3. Turn right on State Forest Road (CR 13). Turn left on Pine Hills Road.
UTM coordinates: 16S, 285880 E, 4154550 N
About the campground: This campground occupies the bottom of a densely wooded ravine that feels far removed from the nearby floodplain farmland. The flat spacious campsites sit under an inviting canopy of oak and pine. Sites are spread out fairly well and are semiprivate. At night, campers may be lulled to sleep by the sound of a rocky-bottomed stream that twists along the backside of many of the sites. A 2-mile hiking trail takes visitors to the dramatic bluffs at the nearby LaRue–Pine Hills Research Natural Area. The natural area is known for its 350-foot bluffs, as well as its biannual "snake migration" across LaRue Road at the base of the bluffs, adjacent to LaRue Swamp. The road is closed to vehicle traffic every spring and fall to help protect thousands of reptiles and amphibians during their migration between their summer and winter habitats.

178 Thebes

Location: On the Mississippi River 8 miles southeast of Cape Girardeau, Missouri
Season: Year-round
Sites: 25 sites with water, electrical, and sewer hookups
Maximum length: 40 feet
Facilities: Tables, fire rings, picnic tables, tables, picnic shelter (no restrooms)
Fee per night: $$
Management: Village of Thebes
Contact: (618) 764-2658; reservations accepted
Finding the campground: Coming from the north on I-57, exit west on IL 146. Pass through Anna and Jonesboro. Turn left on IL 3/146. Before reaching Thebes, turn right on New Route 3. Turn right on Riverview Drive and follow signs to the camping area.
UTM coordinates: 16S, 281456 E, 4121928 N
About the campground: This modest campground claims a fine patch of real estate between the shore of the Mississippi River and a municipal park in the village of Thebes. Maple trees provide some shade for the flat, wide-open camping area. To the left of the campground sits a dramatic three-quarter-mile-long train trestle bridge 100 feet above the river. Behind you perched on the top of the river bluff is a limestone and timber courthouse that was built in 1848 when Thebes

served as the county seat. Dred Scott, the slave who unsuccessfully sued the U.S. government for his freedom, was held as a prisoner here. Call first: The nearby houses built on stilts serve as a tip-off that flooding regularly occurs.

179 Horseshoe Lake State Fish and Wildlife Area

Location: 15 miles northwest of Cairo
Season: Year-round
Sites: 78 sites with electrical hookups, 10 sites with no hookups
Maximum length: 40 feet
Facilities: Tables, grills, flush toilets, showers, water, dump station, nearby boat rentals, playground, picnic shelter
Fee per night: $$–$$$

Stands of cypress, tupelo gum, and swamp cotton trees grow in thick stands within Horseshoe Lake.

Management: Illinois Department of Natural Resources

Contact: (618) 776-5689; http://dnr.state.il.us/lands/Landmgt/parks/r5/horshu.htm

Finding the campground: From I-57 north of Mounds, exit on Mounds Road heading west. Turn left on IL 127, and then turn right on Sycamore Street (CR 6). Turn left on Promised Land Road.

UTM coordinates: 16S, 293471 E, 4109485 N

About the campground: The swamplike appearance of Horseshoe Lake makes one think an alligator will emerge from it at any moment. Despite the look of southern swampland, there's no need to worry about gators. Two campgrounds—one on each side of Horseshoe Lake—put you right up against the shoreline of this 2,400-acre lake containing thick stands of bald cypress, tupelo gum, and swamp cotton trees. The grassy campsites sit on a gentle slope above the water. Maple trees provide ample shade. The open layout allows great views of the lake but affords little privacy. Fishing is the sport of choice here, as is picnicking and lawn-chair relaxation. The center of the lake contains a big island with a loop trail. During winter, 150,000 Canada geese call the lake home.

180 Grand Chain

Location: 20 miles west of Metropolis on the shore of the Ohio River

Season: Year-round

Sites: 25 sites with electrical and sewer hookups, 10 sites water and electrical hookups

Maximum length: 45 feet

Facilities: Tables, grills, flush toilets, showers, water, dump station, playground

Fee per night: $$

Management: Pulaski County Development Association

Contact: (618) 745-6226; (618) 697-0205 for reservations

Finding the campground: From I-57 near Ullin, head east on Ullin Road. Turn right on IL 37. Turn left on Main Street (CR 2) in New Grand Chain. Continue ahead as Main Street turns into Tick Ridge Road. Turn right on Lighthouse Lane.

UTM coordinates: 16S, 325265 E, 4122204 N

About the campground: This basic campground on the shore of the Ohio River caters to RV owners. The camping area is flat with a mix of grass and gravel and offers a minimal amount of shade. A small pond and patches of cropland border the camping area. Grand Chain is a good jumping off point for those who want to explore the Cache River wetlands.

181 Fort Massac State Park

Location: On the outskirts of Metropolis on the shore of the Ohio River
Season: Year-round
Sites: 50 sites with electrical hookups, 7 sites with no hookups
Maximum length: 40 feet
Facilities: Flush toilets, grills, showers, water, picnic areas, dump station, boat launch, visitor center/museum, hiking trails, historic fort replica
Fee per night: $$–$$$
Management: Illinois Department of Natural Resources
Contact: (618) 524-4712; http://dnr.state.il.us/lands/landmgt/parks/r5/frmindex.htm
Finding the campground: From I-24 north of the Ohio River, exit west on US 45. The park appears on the left.
UTM coordinates: 16S, 348320 E, 4112253 N
About the campground: Illinois' first state park is on the shore of the Ohio River at the edge of the town of Metropolis. A replica of a timber fort built in 1802 serves as the centerpiece of the park. Between 1757 and the Civil War, French, English, and U.S. forces each housed troops here. The flat camping area is well shaded with oak and maple trees. The park visitor center has on display a collection of artifacts from the fort as well as a collection of arrowheads. In downtown Metropolis, comic book fans will be delighted with the Superman Museum.

Index

About the Author

Ted Villaire is the author of *60 Hikes within 60 Miles: Chicago* and *Easy Hikes Close to Home: Chicago*. Villaire, a Chicago-based freelance writer, has worked as a news reporter for various daily and weekly newspapers; his freelance articles have appeared in the *Chicago Tribune* and the *Des Moines Register*, among many other publications. He received a bachelor's degree from Aquinas College in Grand Rapids, Michigan, and a master's degree from DePaul University in Chicago. Get in touch with him and check out more photos of the parks and campgrounds featured in this book at www .tedvillaire.com.

COURTESY OF MICHAEL ROBERTS